Jay Boyd Crawford

The Credit Mobilier of America

It's History, Origin, etc.

Jay Boyd Crawford

The Credit Mobilier of America
It's History, Origin, etc.

ISBN/EAN: 9783744692977

Printed in Europe, USA, Canada, Australia, Japan

Cover: Foto ©ninafisch / pixelio.de

More available books at **www.hansebooks.com**

THE
CREDIT MOBILIER

OF AMERICA

ITS ORIGIN AND HISTORY

ITS WORK OF
CONSTRUCTING THE UNION PACIFIC RAILROAD
AND THE RELATION OF

MEMBERS OF CONGRESS THEREWITH

By J. B. CRAWFORD

BOSTON
C. W. CALKINS & CO., PUBLISHERS
1880

Entered according to Act of Congress, in the year 1880, by
C. W. CALKINS & CO.
In the office of the Librarian of Congress, at Washington, D. C.

PRESS OF C. W. CALKINS & CO., BOSTON.

PREFACE.

In presenting this book to the public the author has been led by the hope that it might, in a measure, clear away much of the misunderstanding that has always existed regarding the objects and accomplishments of the Credit Mobilier. For years it has been received, as a fact beyond dispute, that the work of this corporation was one of fraud upon the Government and the people of this country. It has been talked about by almost every one. It has been commented upon in the press and before the public until its name has become a familiar sound in almost every household in the land. In all this controversy there has been one uniform opinion, and that opinion has been entertained almost unanimously by the the public. Not less was the author at one time impressed with this same general idea. He, in common with nearly all others, believed that those who had carried on this work had used their power and influence to grow rich at the expense of the government. As he read the reports, which had been submitted to Congress by the committees of investigation, still more firmly did he find that opinion impressed upon his mind. A careful reading of the testimony upon which those reports were based, led to the conviction that an almost fatal error had been committed, and that the judgment which had been rendered by the public was one not supported by the evidence, and which would never have been pronounced had an opportunity been given for the consideration of the truth. The judicial investigations that have been accorded by the courts have done much to remove the doubts of many, and to give a clearer insight into the true relations of the most gigantic achievement of the present century.

Time had in a great measure overcome the feeling against the Credit Mobilier, but during the past few months the interest has revived and the public were anxious to know the truth. The object of this book is to furnish that information. How well that object has been accomplished the public must judge. The author has attempted to deal impartially, to give credit only where it is due, and censure only where merited. The work is not designed as a political work in any sense; the great blessings that have accrued to the nation through the construction of that great highway have carried the work of the Credit Mobilier above and beyond the sphere of politics, and it is hoped that when the truth shall become known the public will not, alone comprehend but approve that work.

J. B. C.

Oct. 15, 1880.

CONTENTS.

I.
THE ORIGIN OF THE COMPANY 9

II.
THE ACT OF INCORPORATION 17

III.
THE UNION PACIFIC RAILROAD COMPANY 24

IV.
THE AMES CONTRACT AND ASSIGNMENT 38

V.
THE ASSIGNMENT TO SEVEN TRUSTEES 55

VI.
THE DIFFICULTIES OF CONSTRUCTION 73

VII.
THE DISAGREEMENT WITH MR. McCOMB 88

VIII.
THE POLLAND COMMITTEE 121

IX.
DEFENCE OF OAKES AMES 186

X.
THE VOTE OF CENSURE 214

XI.
THE CREDIT MOBILIER OF TO-DAY 220

THE CREDIT MOBILIER

OF AMERICA.

I.

THE ORIGIN OF THE COMPANY.

SOME eight years ago the country was startled by the announcement of the grossest corruption in our national legislature, arising out of the building of the Union Pacific Railroad, and which involved the names of many of the most prominent men in Congress—men whose reputation had before been above suspicion—men whose record had always been spotless. The news came with terrible force upon the community. The time—that of a presidential election—was one well calculated to add force to the calamity that had seemingly overtaken our country. The name of "Credit Mobilier," until then almost unknown and unheard of except among a few, now came into most wonderful prominence, and to this day, though spoken of by everyone, has remained a mystery. The name, with its foreign sound, was one well calculated to raise additional alarm, and was one which politicians could handle with ease to instil into the minds of the people ideas of great corruption. Why should such a name be selected if the purposes of that corporation were honorable ? and they who wished to use it lost no opportunity of doing so; and yet it is safe to say that not one in a thousand of those who dwelt upon the infamy of the Credit Mobilier had the faintest conception of what it really was, what were its objects, or what it had accomplished. But that could not deter them in their argument; they knew its purposes were not honest, and that was enough for them. It was as the cloud, small at first, but soon the tempest that arose was sufficient to destroy all that came within its reach. Reputations which had been towers of strength were suddenly overwhelmed and covered with infamy; they who had been the leaders of public opinion and of public morals were swept away in the maelstrom of public condemnation, never again to regain their position. So great was that condemnation by the people of the acts of these men that in an evil moment they sought to regain their lost positions by denying all connection with, or interest in, the Credit Mobilier; not stopping to consider whether that connection was good or evil, but listening only to the clamors of the present, they sought to shield themselves behind the armor of their hitherto unquestioned word; but alas! when revelation came, and that word was found to be false, the last defence was gone, and they fell. Years have passed, but still those names have been enshrouded by the mystery in which they had fallen. Time has indeed cleared away much of the superstition that was created; but the people, as a mass, remain in ignorance of the real object and workings of the Credit Mobilier. What was it? What did it accomplish? These are questions that are daily and hourly asked by the many. Let them but go out beyond the Missouri, upon the Great American Desert of a score of years ago, and behold the mighty empire that has sprung into existence there; behold the towns and cities teeming with population, farms that supply the world with bread, homes provided with every comfort and luxury of life; behold on every side the school-houses where children grow up amid the influence of popular education, and as they behold this happy, contented, and enlightened people, strong in their love of freedom and equality, firm in their faith and allegiance to their country—there they may see some of the results that have been accomplished through the influence and instrumentality of those who guided and governed the Credit Mobilier. In a word, the Credit Mobilier and the Union Pacific Railroad Company were one and the same. The men who governed the one, governed the other. Whatever was done under the name of Credit Mobilier may not be known to the world in its true light, but we hope that the facts concerning it may be made to appear upon a perusal of this work. It is not our intention to accuse or apologize for any one, but only to set forth as clearly as we can the history of the

Credit Mobilier of America and its connection with the building of the Union Pacific Railroad, and the relation of members of Congress with it.

The excitement of the past is gone, in a great measure, and the people of the present are prepared to far more impartially judge of the merits or the evils of its operation, and to decide whether the actions of those men were right or wrong. That any crime was ever committed was not a necessary conclusion to be drawn from the revelations that have been made public. Time, and time only, can effectually clear away the clouds of suspicion that have so long hung over many a once-honored name, and only the impartial judgment of history can give complete vindication to those who have been accused. A new generation is fast appearing upon the arena of life, which will be prepared to judge without the feelings of prejudice that have, and may long continue to control public opinion.

Only a short time ago there appeared in the press throughout the country a statement by the sons of Oakes Ames in relation to the association of their father with the Credit Mobilier, which, in connection with the present political campaign, has centred upon this matter an interest before unfelt, and has created an almost universal desire on the part of the public to know more concerning the history of that corporation. Was it a work, as they allege, of such great importance? Was it so largely beneficial to the country that, instead of the odium and disgrace that was cast upon its principal character, a monument should be erected to his memory by a grateful people? No fact is, or can be made more plain, than that no man had so much to do with the success of the building of the Union Pacific Railroad as did Oakes Ames. To his wonderful exertions, to the great sacrifices which he made, is due the building of that road. He assumed the responsibility, and shirked not the ordeal through which he passed. The road was completed, the whole country was benefited, and the union of our states made more strong than ever before; but to Oakes Ames the result was disastrous in the extreme. He was censured by the Congress of which he was a member, and the disgrace which was placed upon him ended his life in a few short months.

A proper study of the Credit Mobilier will make necessary a consideration of the circumstances which called it into existence; and to do this, we shall be compelled to go over the history of the building of the Union Pacific Railroad. The Credit Mobilier, as it came into prominence, was the construction company that took the contract for building the road. Owing to the same parties being the stockholders in the road and the stockholders in the Credit Mobilier it could not well take the contract direct from the Railroad Company, but the contracts came through the intervention of a third party. All this will be seen in the pages which follow, and need not be further alluded to here. Upon the organization of the Union Pacific Railroad Company, under the act of Congress of 1862, and as amended by act of

Congress in 1864, an attempt had been made by that company to construct the road, which effort proved to be a failure, not only because of the lack of confidence which the public had in the scheme, and refusal to invest in the bonds and stock of the company, but their own lack of means, and the responsibilities which such construction cast upon those who undertook it. It was impossible for the company to obtain any individual to take a contract, as no one was willing to shoulder so great an obligation as he must. It was therefore necessary that some means be used by which there could be a combination of capital and at the same time a limit to the liability of losses. It was therefore determined to use the influence of a construction company. Questions of course arose, as to the legality of the proceedings as contemplated, but under the instruction and advice of the most eminent counsel in the world the plan, as carried out, was commenced, carried on, and finished.

The Credit Mobilier of America, which was the name adopted for the company selected for the work, was fashioned after the Credit Mobilier of France, which had long been known in that country. The Credit Mobilier of France was a joint stock company founded in Paris November 18, 1852, under the lead of the brothers Emile and Isaac Péreire, and on the principle of limited liability, for the transaction of general banking business, to facilitate the construction of public works, and to develop internal industry. Its capital was 60,000,000 francs, divided into shares of 500 francs. It was authorized to hold public and other securities, and to issue bonds of its own to an amount equal to its subscriptions and purchases, and after its original capital was all taken, to issue bonds to ten times that amount. The profits of the company were at first very large, a dividend of forty-one per cent. was declared in 1855, and from that down to five per cent. In 1867, having for some years paid only slight dividends (though the average annual dividend for fifteen years was seventeen per cent.), it lost confidence, and the stock fell to twenty-eight per cent. of its par value, and the company soon went into liquidation. The managers retired with immense fortunes. The High Court of Appeals decided (August 1, 1868,) that the brothers Péreire and other directors were responsible for their acts, and that damages should be given to the stockholders. Among the enterprises achieved by the Credit Mobilier of France may be mentioned the construction of the Paris Gas Company, the Paris Omnibus Company, the creation of the company of the Grand Hôtel du Louvre, and of the Maritime Company of Clippers, and immense railway operations in Austria, Spain, Russia, and Switzerland, together with heavy loans to French railway companies. The company met with much opposition, and was at times called the greatest gambling house the world had ever seen.

The Credit Mobilier of America was originally a company organized under the laws of the State of Pennsylvania, in the year 1859, and was then known by the name of The Pennsylvania Fiscal Agency. Under this name, however, it languished, and was not, until shortly previous to its purchase by the principal parties interested in the Union Pacific Railroad, even organized as a corporation. And after its final organization it never called any of its powers or functions into action while it retained its first name. The powers granted to it were of a peculiar nature, and were what were so much needed in the field in which it was soon to appear, that every necessary object was amply provided for. That a full understanding of its provisions may be had, the act in full will be given.

II.

THE ACT OF INCORPORATION.

AN ACT TO INCORPORATE THE PENNSYLVANIA FISCAL AGENCY.

Be it enacted by the senate and house of representatives of the Commonwealth of Pennsylvania in general assembly met, and it is hereby enacted by the authority of the same:

SECTION 1. That Samuel J. Reeves, Ellis Lewis, Garrick Mallory, Duff Green, David R. Porter, Jacob Ziegler, Charles M. Hall, Horn R. Kneass, Robert J. Ross, William T. Dougherty, Isaac Hugus, C. M. Reed, William Workman, Asa Packer, Jesse Lazear, C. S. Kauffman, C. L. Ward, and Henry M. Fuller, be, and they are hereby, appointed commissioners to receive subscriptions and to organize a company, by the name and style of the Pennsylvania Fiscal Agency; and the owners of the shares herein authorized to be issued, when the company is organized, shall, under the name and style aforesaid, have perpetual succession; and may purchase, hold and acquire, by any lawful means, estate real and personal, and the same may use, sell, lease, let, mortgage, transfer, and convey, and otherwise dispose of; and may sue and be sued, plead and be impleaded, contract and be contracted with, and have and use a common seal, and the same may change at pleasure; and may make by-laws and regulations for the government of their affairs, and may have and use all the rights, powers, and privileges which are or may be necessary for them to have as a company incorporated for the powers herein stated: *Provided*, that the said company shall not at any time hold, in this State, more land than may be requisite for the convenient transaction of their business.

Sec. 2. That the purpose of this act is to organize an incorporated company, and to authorize them, as such, to become an agency for the purchase and sale of railroad bonds and other securities, and to make advances of money and of credit to railroad and other improvement companies, and to aid in like manner contractors and manufacturers, and to authorize them, as a company, to make all requisite contracts, and especially to receive and hold, on deposit and in trust, estate, real and personal, including the notes, bonds, obligations, and accounts of states, and of individuals, and of companies, and of corporations, and the same to purchase, collect, adjust, and settle, and also to sell and dispose thereof in any market in the United States, or elsewhere, without proceedings in law, or in equity, and for such price and on such terms as may be agreed on between them and the parties contracting with them, and also to endorse and guarantee the payment of the bonds and the performance of the obligations of individuals, of corporations, and of companies.

Sec. 3. That the capital stock of said company shall consist of fifty thousand shares of $100 each;

and the commissioners aforesaid, or a majority of them, may, in person or by proxy, open books of subscription at such times and places as they deem expedient, and when five thousand shares shall have been subscribed, and five per cent. thereon shall have been paid in, the shareholders may elect five or more directors; and the directors of the said company, when it shall have been organized, may, and they are hereby authorized and empowered, to have and to exercise, in the name and behalf of the company, all the rights, powers, and privileges which are intended to be herein given; and may, from time to time, increase their resources by borrowing money on a pledge of their property, or without such pledge, or by new subscriptions, not exceeding fifty thousand shares; and any citizen or subject, company or corporation, of any State or county, may subscribe for, purchase, and hold shares of the said company, with all the rights, and subject only to such liabilities as other shareholders are subject to; which liabilities are no more than for the payment to the company of the sums due, or to become due, on the shares held by them; and when new subscriptions are made, the shares may be issued at par, or sold for the benefit of the holders of the shares heretofore issued.

SEC. 4. That the by-laws shall prescribe the manner in which the officers and agents of the company shall be chosen, and designate their powers and duties, and their terms of service and compensation; and the principal office of the company shall be in Philadelphia, but the directors, under such rules and regulations as they may prescribe, may establish branches and agencies in Europe and elsewhere, and may deal in exchange, foreign and domestic; but the said company shall not exercise the privileges of banking, nor issue their own notes or bills to be used as bank-notes or as currency.

SEC. 5. That three-fifths of the directors of said company shall be citizens of the United States, and the majority of the whole shall reside in this State.

SEC. 6. That the said company shall pay to the State treasurer, for the use of the State, a bonus of one-half of one per cent. on the sum requisite to be paid in previous to the organization, payable in four equal annual instalments, the first payment to be made in one year after the payment on the capital stock shall be made, and also a like bonus on all subsequent payments on account of the capital stock of the said company, or any increase thereof, payable in like manner; and, in addition to such bonus, shall pay such tax upon the dividends exceeding six per cent. per annum as is or may be imposed by law.

W. C. A. LAWRENCE,
Speaker of the House of Representatives.

JNO. CRESWELL, JR.,
Speaker of the Senate.

Approved the first day of November, anno Domini one thousand eight hundred and fifty-nine.

WM. F. PACKER.

Such is the original act of incorporation of the famous Credit Mobilier of America, and under this act the organization of the company was concluded, and officers duly elected. The first election of directors took place on the 29th of May, 1863, and the first officers of the corporation were Jacob Zeigler, president; Oliver Barnes, secretary; and Charles M. Hall, treasurer. The history of the company under this organization was not of great importance, but it was destined soon to assume a place in the national history of our republic, and call to itself the attention of the whole world.

On the third day of March, 1864, Thomas C. Durant, then vice-president of the Union Pacific Railroad Company, purchased the charter of the Pennsylvania Fiscal Agency for the purpose of using the company for the construction of the Union Pacific Railroad. But great changes were in store for the Fiscal Agency. On the twenty-sixth of March, 1864, only twenty-three days from the purchase, the following act passed the Pennsylvania legislature :

AN ACT TO CHANGE THE NAME OF THE PENNSYLVANIA FISCAL AGENCY.

Be it enacted by the senate and house of representatives of the Commonwealth of Pennsylvania, in general assembly met, and it is hereby enacted by the authority of the same:

That from and after the passage of this act "The Pennsylvania Fiscal Agency" shall be named instead thereof "The Credit Mobilier of America", with all the powers, privileges, and authorities they had under their former name, and be subject to all the restrictions and liabilities to which they were subject under the same.

HENRY C. JOHNSON,
Speaker of the House of Representatives.

JOHN P. PENNEY,
Speaker of the Senate.

Approved the twenty-sixth day of March, anno Domini one thousand eight hundred and sixty-four.

A. G. CURTIN.

But the change in name was one of slight importance with what followed. Under the provisions of the charter an agency was established in the city of New York, and when subscriptions to the Company were made it was upon the express condition that the full powers of the board of directors should be given to the New York agency; it was also stipulated that a railroad bureau should be established at the New York agency, of five managers; three to be directors of the Company, who should have the sole management of railway contracts, subject however to the approval of the president of the Company. The number of managers was afterwards increased to seven. By these means the Pennsylvania corporation, with name changed, removed itself, so far as the management of its affairs was concerned, entirely from the state of Pennsylvania, maintaining there only its corporate existence, and with the extraordinary powers conferred upon it by that state, took upon itself the construction of the Union Pacific Railroad Company.

At this time the outstanding stock of the Union Pacific Railroad Company amounted to $2,180,000, upon which there had been made to the Railroad Company a payment of ten per cent. or $218.000. This stock was purchased by the Credit Mobilier, by repaying to the stockholders the amount advanced by them — that is $218.000. When the Credit Mobilier purchased this Union Pacific stock the par value of the shares was $1000. By act of Congress of 1864, this stock was cancelled and a reissue was made to the stockholders of the Credit Mobilier in shares of $100; and thus the stockholders of the two corporations became identical; the stockholders in each taking *pro rata* with his interest in the other, and thus the persons composing one corporation, who were to take a contract to build the road, were the very same persons who held complete control of the corporation for which the road was to be built.

III.

THE UNION PACIFIC RAILROAD CO.

LET us turn for a few moments to a consideration of the status of the Union Pacific Railroad at this time, and to do this it will be necessary to investigate briefly the circumstances which made that work a national necessity. Twenty years ago had any one advocated the building of such a road, he would have been looked upon as insane. Yet we find that the discovery of gold on the Pacific coast attracted there a large population who, separated as they were from the influence of the rest of our country, were gradually acquiring a sentiment of independence toward the common country; and the conclusion was coming slowly but surely that their interests, separated by so great a distance from the East, could be best protected in a nation governed by their own peculiar laws; and at the breaking out of the great civil war, there was danger of our losing that valuable territory west of the Rocky mountains unless some means could be devised to place them in closer communication with the East; and to do this it would be necessary to construct a railroad across the entire country and thus, by placing them in easy access to the East, strengthen the bonds of union between the Atlantic and Pacific coast, develop the immense resources of the central portion of the United States, and open a new route for commerce from the Atlantic and Europe, to the Pacific and Asia. This was an idea that came uppermost in the minds of the government during even the first years of the great war. Every effort was made to secure this end; every means was tried to induce capitalists to embark their fortunes in the undertaking. The government in July, 1862, incorporated the company, giving them vast grants of land along the entire route, loaning them government bonds to a large amount per mile of the road, and asking only that its loan should constitute a first lien upon the road when completed. Books for subscriptions to the stock were opened throughout the country, but the undertaking was too hazardous and novel to secure the co-operation of any responsible persons, and during the following two years only $2,180,000 of the stock was subscribed for, and only ten per cent. of that amount was actually paid in in cash. Thus it will be seen that, in spite of all the concessions and aid that the government tendered, only $218,000 had been raised to complete this vast work. One restriction which the government had imposed, was that the capital stock of the company, which was placed at $100,000,000, should not be sold at less than par, or $100 per share. In order to have enabled any company to obtain the control of the road would have required an investment of some $51,000,000.

In July, 1864, Congress deemed it necessary to increase the inducement for capital to embark in this great enterprise, and therefore it doubled the land grant, and authorized the company to issue an equal amount of first mortgage bonds, having precedence over those of the government; thus in reality reducing the lien of the government for the bonds advanced by it, to a second mortgage. This course led to practical action. In the meantime however, attempts had been made to build the Union Pacific Railroad. Immediately after the first organization of the company in 1862, they went to work and commenced to build the road themselves by putting men and laborers on. This was continued through the fall and winter of 1863 and 1864, by which time the company had expended upwards of $600,000, leaving the company in debt beyond the subscriptions received by them, of $281,000, to the amount of more than $300,000. They found it impossible to proceed with the work; parties would not take the stock, and they were forced to sell some of the materials, cars, &c., which they had bought; and yet they did not entirely abandon the work.

May 12, 1864, a committee was appointed with authority to receive proposals and let the work of building the road to private parties. A contract was made with H. M. Hoxie, August 8th, 1864, for the construction of one hundred miles of road, commencing at the city of Omaha, at the rate of $50,000 for each and every mile so completed; the contractor to receive the securities of the company in payment. It was but a short time after Hoxie had taken this contract that he found he could not go on with it, and he assigned his contract to the Credit Mobilier, which corporation only a few months before had been obtained by the principal stockholders of the Union Pacific Railroad for the very purpose of taking the contract of constructing the road; and doubtless the contract to Hoxie was only for the purpose of having it assigned. The date of that assignment was March 15, 1865; but as early as October 7, 1864, an agreement was made between said Hoxie and Thomas C. Durant, president of the Credit Mobilier, and who was also vice-president of the Union Pacific Railroad Company, that such an assignment should be made to such party or parties as said Durant should name. One condition of the contract of Hoxie was that he should subscribe for the capital stock of the Union Pacific Railroad to the amount of $500,000. Only three days prior to the agreement to assign, and at a time when Hoxie had virtually abandoned his contract, if indeed he had ever taken it in good faith, the following correspondence passed between the two parties:

NEW YORK, October 4, 1864.

To the President and Executive Committee of the Union Pacific Railroad Company:

On condition that your railroad company will extend my contract from its present length of 100 miles, so as to embrace all that portion of the road between Omaha and the 100th meridian of longitude, I will subscribe, or cause to be subscribed for, $500,000 of the stock of your company.

H. M. Hoxie,
By H. C. Crane,
Attorney.

The above proposition is hereby accepted for and on behalf of the Union Pacific Railroad Company.

John A. Dix,
C. S. Bushnell,
Geo. T. M. Davis.
Special Committee.

October 3, 1864.

Thus the Hoxie contract was made to embrace all the road between Omaha and the one hundredth meridian, a distance of $247\frac{45}{100}$ miles, and three days later this contract was virtually assigned to the Credit Mobilier, though in form the assignment was made in the following March, and the Credit Mobilier, under this assignment, completed the contract on the fifth of October, 1866.

It was alleged by some of the witnesses before the Congressional committee that this contract cost the Union Pacific Railroad Company $12,974,416.24, and that it cost the Credit Mobilier 7,806,183.33, being a profit to the Credit Mobilier of $5,168,-232.91. This alleged profit, it should be borne in mind, was in stock and bonds of the Union Pacific Railroad Company estimated at par, while the market value of the stock was only about thirty cents, and of the bonds about eighty-five cents on the dollar. The facts concerning this profit will be spoken of further on.

The contract with Hoxie having been completed, a new agreement was made by Thomas C. Durant, vice-president of the Union Pacific Railroad, with a Mr. Boomer, for the construction of $153\tfrac{38}{100}$ miles of road west from the one hundredth meridian. Under this agreement Boomer was to receive $19,500 per mile for that portion of the contract east of the North Platte, and for that portion of the contract west of the river $20,000 per mile—the bridge across the river, station buildings, equipment, etc., to be additional. This contract was never ratified by the company, although some fifty-eight miles of the road had been completed. It has been impossible to ascertain what these fifty-eight miles cost the company, but from the evidence of Mr. Durant, the only evidence attainable, it appears that it did not exceed $27,500 per mile, including station houses, equipments, etc. Yet in view of all this, and with the facts clearly before the company, on the fifth of January, 1867, the board of directors, by a resolution, extended the Hoxie contract over these fifty-eight miles, thus proposing to pay to the Credit Mobilier—the Credit Mobilier being in reality themselves—$22,500 per mile for these fifty-eight miles (amounting to $1,345,000) without any consideration whatever, the road already having been completed and accepted by the government.

The following is a copy of the resolution, of date January 5, 1867.

Resolved, That the Union Pacific Railroad Company will, and do hereby consider the Hoxie contract extended to the point already completed, namely, 305 miles west from Omaha, and that the officers of this company are hereby authorized to settle with the Credit Mobilier at $50,000 per mile for the additional fifty-eight miles.

This resolution was not carried out on account of the protest against it by Thomas C. Durant, although, as will appear hereafter, this road, fully constructed and accepted by the government, costing in its construction, according to the statement of Mr. Durant, though no record of it could be found on the books of the railroad company, complete, with station houses, equipment, etc., not over $27,500 per mile, was included in the Ames contract, which will soon be outlined, and paid for there at the rate of $42,000 per mile.

The reader will more clearly understand the true relations of this extension of the contract, and the position of Mr. Durant concerning it, when he has been informed that, at about this time, Mr. Durant had been removed from the board of directors of the Credit Mobilier, and that a desperate quarrel had ensued, in which he openly made his boasts that the Credit Mobilier should never have another contract from the Union Pacific Railroad. The dissensions that arose concerning this were of long duration, and entailed immense difficulties upon both companies.

From the evidence that has been produced, it has also appeared that the contract with Boomer, just alluded to, never had any existence, except in the mind of Mr. Durant; that the work upon these fifty-eight miles had, in fact, been performed by the Credit Mobilier, under the expectation of receiving the contract for its construction. The Credit Mobilier had gone on with the work, had expended its money in its construction, and, when it became apparent that the opposition of Durant and his party was strong enough to prevent the execution of the contract, the board of directors of the railroad, in doing what they supposed to be only just and fair, voted to extend the Hoxie contract over these fifty-eight miles, in order that the Credit Mobilier might receive returns for their expenses. Mr. Durant then protested against this action of the board, for the reason, as it afterwards appeared, of having it a matter of record, to which he could subsequently refer, to show the purity of his motives, should any investigation ever be made. In spite of the failure of this extension of the contract, owing to the friendly attitude of the railway company toward the Credit Mobilier, and the promise to give them a contract as soon as possible, the Credit Mobilier continued to construct the road, even beyond the fifty-eight miles above spoken of.

On the first of March, 1867, another contract was made, for building the road west of the one hundredth meridian, to J. M. S. Williams. This contract was to cover $267\tfrac{53}{100}$ miles, at a cost of \$50,000 per mile, and included that portion which was already completed; but at this time the completed portion of the road west of the one hundredth meridian, to be included in this contract, extended over ninety-eight and one-fourth miles. This proposition was accepted by the company with the proviso: "That $7,500 per mile be reserved out of the payment." At the time of making this contract, Williams had made an agreement with the Credit Mobilier that he would assign his contract to them. Thus in reality making the contract between the Union Pacific Railroad and the Credit Mobilier; that is, a contract to the Credit Mobilier, by which they were to receive payment for the road which was already completed, at the same rate as under the Hoxie contract. This contract of Williams was not, however, carried out, owing to the protest of Mr. Durant, which protest can best be understood by reading the same, which is in the words following:—

UNION PACIFIC RAILROAD OFFICE,

March 27, 1867.

To the Directors of the Union Pacific Railroad Company:

GENTLEMEN,—I protest against the resolution of the board of directors, passed at your last meeting, which proposes to give the contract of the road of this company, commencing at the one hundredth meridian of longitude, for the reason that a section of road, already accepted, is included in the contract, and it does not appear that this company derives any benefit adequate to the price paid over the cost of construction, and does not in future require, as an essential point in the contract, the completion of the road within the shortest possible time, and for other reasons named in a previous protest, in relation to the Hoxie contract.

I beg to call your attention again to the fact that part of this work has been done for weeks, and that contracts have been made, and merchandise delivered, for nearly one hundred and fifty miles of road, which the company has paid for, as shown by the books.

Respectfully,

THOMAS C. DURANT.

The next important step in the history of this transaction is the Ames contract, the most important, perhaps, of any that was made during the construction of this great road. But, before touching on that, it may be well to dwell a little on the relations of these different corporations, that is, the Union Pacific Railroad and the Credit Mobilier.

It must be borne in mind that the stockholders of the one and the stockholders of the other were identical, and that whatever contracts were made by the one were known to the other. The first large contract that was made was with H. M. Hoxie, and it may be interesting to inquire, who was Hoxie? The contract which he had taken implied not merely an expenditure of many millions of dollars in the construction of the road, which was to be repaid him in the securities of the company, but a subscription of $500,000 in stock of the Railroad. These securities could not easily be converted into cash, even far below par, thus making it an outlay of cash essentially.

Who was this man with such unlimited means? The testimony of Mr. Oliver Ames before the Congressional committee is that Hoxie was a man of no responsibility; that he was an employé of the road, and had charge of the ferry over the Missouri river at Omaha; that it was never expected that he would carry out the contract; that he was simply a figure-head; a party to whom the contract was to be let with the view of his turning it over to some one else. That some one else proved to be the Credit Mobilier—the very parties who under the guise of a different name, let the contract to him. The same is also true of the contracts with Boomer, and the one made later with Davis. Was it all the same with the immense contract of Mr. Ames, which was next to follow? We shall have occasion to consider this farther on. Up to this time, then, there had been built over three hundred miles of this road, and the construction was by the Credit Mobilier. Where did this corporation get all these means? They took their pay from the Union Pacific Railroad Company, in the stocks and bonds of the road, and it became necessary to convert these into cash. They could not buy, nor could the directors of the railroad sell the stock of the road for less than par; and when it was placed upon the market it would not bring more than thirty cents on the dollar, and few sales could be made even at that or any other price.

The road could not issue it for less than par, and so the Credit Mobilier must lose at least seventy dollars on every share of the stock that they purchased. It must appear upon the records of the Railroad Company that this stock was paid for in cash; that was required by the articles of incorporation. They could not use it to pay for the construction of their road. The act of incorporation required that it should be sold for cash at not less than par. But through the influence of the Credit Mobilier, they were enabled not only to evade one of these requirements, but both. They not only by this means used the stock and bonds of the road, but also sold the stock of the same far below par. The plan of operations, briefly stated, was that when any payment was to be made on account of work done, the Railroad Company would give its check to the Credit Mobilier for the amount, and thereupon the Credit Mobilier would pass the identical check back to the Railroad Company, receiving from them the stock and bonds. This they called a cash transaction; and yet the Union Pacific Railroad Company had no money, except as they sold their stock or bonds, or converted the government loans into cash. The Credit Mobilier had no money, except as they sold these stocks and bonds; for their capital, originally of $2,500,000, afterwards increased to $3,750,000, was soon used up in the construction of this road. But to all intents and purposes, the two companies were one and the same. Even this position was claimed by Thomas C. Durant, the president of the Credit Mobilier, and this was one ground of his objection to the extension of the Hoxie contract.

Durant was opposed to the Credit Mobilier, as a corporation, having any further contracts with the Railroad Company, and it was not strange that such should be the case. Gradually large amounts of the stock of the Railroad Company had been absorbed by the public, and unless some means were taken to secure to themselves the benefits of these great contracts, they might lose their advantage. Some more stringent means must be used; something must be done by which the control of the two corporations should remain undisturbed and secure, until the mission of the Credit Mobilier should be accomplished, and this was done most effectually in the next great move in the history of this road.

After the proposition of J. M. S. Williams was made, no great change occurred in the situation of affairs. In spite of the allegations to the contrary, the testimony of the many witnesses before the Congressional committee was, that work was constantly being done upon the road, and by the 16th of August, 1867 — the date of the Ames contract — one hundred and thirty-eight miles of the road west of the one-hundredth meridian had been completed and accepted by the government, and this construction had been done at an expense, on an average, including equipments, of about $27,000 per mile, to the Company. Still let us bear in mind that the only evidence of the cost of this portion of the road rests on the testimony of Mr. Durant, and that the books of the Railroad Company do not give any evidence of this cost.

The Oakes Ames contract, of which we shall now speak, was for the construction of 667 miles of road, commencing at the one-hundredth meridian, at prices ranging from $42,000 per mile, for the first hundred miles, to $96,000 per mile. It has been alleged by some, that there was an understanding between the officers of these two companies, that this contract, known as the Ames contract, should be assigned by him for the benefit of the Credit Mobilier. By others it was claimed that it was only an implied understanding. But the facts show that reliance was placed solely upon the honor of Mr. Ames to make the assignment for the benefit of all. However this may be, whether the understanding was expressed or implied, or whether there was no understanding at all, it is hardly material; for within two months from the signing of the contract by Mr. Ames, it was assigned to seven persons as trustees, for the benefit of the stockholders of the Credit Mobilier. We shall consider the nature of this assignment a little further on. These trustees were among the principal stockholders and directors of the Credit Mobilier and the Union Pacific Railroad Company, and under their direction, that portion of the Union Pacific Railroad embraced in the Ames contract was completed.

That this contract may be fully understood, as well as the assignment to the trustees, they will each be set out in full.

IV.

THE AMES CONTRACT AND ASSIGNMENT.

THE OAKES AMES CONTRACT.

AGREEMENT made this 16th day of August, 1867, between the Union Pacific Railroad Company, party of the first part, and Oakes Ames, party of the second part, witnesseth —

That the party of the first part agrees to let and contract, and the party of the second part agrees to contract, as follows, to wit:

First. The party of the second part agrees and binds himself, his heirs, executors, administrators, and assigns, to build and equip the following-named portions of the railroad and telegraph line of the party of the first part, commencing at the 100th meridian of longitude, upon the following terms and conditions, to wit:

1st 100 miles at, and for the rate of $42,000 per mile.
2d 167 miles at, and for the rate of $45,000 per mile.
3d 100 miles at, and for the rate of $96,000 per mile.
4th 100 miles at, and for the rate of $80,000 per mile.
5th 100 miles at, and for the rate of $90,000 per mile.
6th 100 miles at, and for the rate of $96,000 per mile.

Second. At least 350 miles shall be, if possible, completed and ready for acceptance before the 1st day of January, 1868, provided the Union Pacific Railroad Company transport the material. The whole to be constructed in a good and workmanlike manner, upon the same general plan and specifications as adopted east of the 100th meridian of longitude. The party of the second part shall erect all such necessary depots, machine-shops, machinery, tanks, turn-tables, and provide all necessary machinery and rolling-stock, at a cost of not less than $7,500 per mile, in cash, and shall construct all such necessary side-track as may be required by the party of the first part, not exceeding six per cent. of the length of the road constructed, and to be constructed under this contract. The kind of timber used for ties, and in the bridges, and in its preparation, shall be such as from time to time may be ordered or prescribed by the general agent, or the company, under the rules and regulations, and standard as recommended by the Secretary of the Interior of the date of February ——, 1866.

Third. Whenever one of the above-named sections of the road shall be finished to the satisfaction and acceptance of the Government Commissioners, the same shall be delivered into the possession of the party of the first part, and upon such portions of the road, as well as on that part east of the 100th meridian now completed, the party of the first part shall transport, without delay, all men and material, to be used in construction, at a price to be agreed upon by the party of the second part, his heirs, executors, administrators, or assigns, and the general agent, but not less than cost to the party of the first part.

Fourth. The party of the second part, his heirs, executors, administrators, or assigns, shall have the right to enter upon all lands belonging to the company, or upon which the company may have any rights, and take therefrom any material used in the construction of the road, and may have the right to change the grade and curvature within the limits of the provisions of the act of Congress, for the temporary purpose of hastening the completion of the road, but the estimated cost of reducing the same to the grade and curvatures, as established by the chief engineer, or as approved from time to time by the company, shall be deducted and retained by the party of the first part, until such grade and curvature is so reduced.

Fifth. The party of the second part, his heirs, executors, administrators, or assigns, is to receive from the company, and enjoy the benefit of all existing contracts, and shall assume all such contracts, and all liabilities of the company accrued or arising therefrom for work done, or to be done, and material furnished, or to be furnished, for or on account of the road west of the 100th meridian, crediting, however, the party of the first part on this contract all moneys heretofore paid or expended on account thereof.

Sixth. The party of the second part, for himself, his heirs, executors, administrators, and assigns, stipulates and agrees, that the work shall be prosecuted and completed with energy and all possible speed, so as to complete the same at the earliest practicable day, it being understood that the speed of construction and time of completion is the essence of this contract, and at the same time the road to be a first-class road, with equipments; and if the same, in the opinion of the chief engineer, is not so prosecuted, both as regards quality and dispatch, that then the said party of the first part shall, and may, through its general agent, or other officer detailed for that purpose, take charge of said work, and carry the same on at proper cost and expense of the party of the second part.

Seventh. The grading, bridging, and superstructure to be completed under the supervision of the general agent of the company, to the satisfaction of the chief engineer, and to be of the same character as to the workmanship and materials as in the construction of the road east of the 100th meridian.

It is, however, understood that all iron hereafter purchased or contracted for, shall be of the weight of not less than fifty-six pounds to the yard, and to be fish-bar joints.

Eighth. All the expenses of the engineering are to be charged and paid by the party of the second part, except the pay and salary of the chief engineer and consulting engineer, and their immediate assistants, and the expenses of the general survey of the route.

Ninth. The depot buildings, machine-shops, water-tanks, and also bridges, shall be of the most approved pattern, and they, as well as the kind of masonry and other material used, shall be previously approved by the general agent and chief engineer of the company, and all tunnels shall be of the proper width for a double track, and shall be arched with brick or stone, when necessary, for the protection of the same.

Tenth. Payments to be made as the work progresses, upon the estimates of the chief engineer, — in making which the engineer shall deduct from each section its proportionate cost of the equipment not then furnished, station-buildings, superstructure, and cost of telegraph; but all materials delivered or in transit for the account of the company, may be estimated for.

Eleventh. Payments hereon shall be made to the party of the second part, his heirs, executors, administrators, or assigns, in cash; but if the government bonds received by the company cannot be converted into money at their par value net, and the first mortgage bonds of the company, at ninety cents on the dollar net, then the said party of the second part, his heirs, executors, administrators, and assigns, shall be charged herein the difference between the amount realized and the above-named rates; provided the first mortgage bonds are not sold for less than eighty cents on the dollar; and if there shall not be realized from the sale of such bonds an amount sufficient to pay the party of the second part, his heirs, executors, administrators, or assigns, for work as stipulated in this contract, and according to the terms thereof, then such deficiency shall, from time to time, be subscribed by said party of the second part, his heirs, executors, administrators, or assigns, to the capital stock of said company, and proceeds of such subscriptions shall be paid to said party of the second part, his heirs, executors, administrators, or assigns, on this contract.

Twelfth. On the first one hundred miles on this contract, there shall be added to the equipment now provided for, and intended to apply on this section, as follows, viz. : six locomotives, fifty box-cars, four passenger-cars, two baggage-cars, and a proportionate amount of equipment of like character, to be supplied on the second section of one hundred miles after the same is completed.

Thirteenth. The amount provided to be expended for equipment, station-buildings, &c., shall be expended under the direction of the party of the first part, and in such proportion for cars, locomotives, machine-shops, station-buildings, &c., and at such points as they may determine. The party of the first part to have the full benefit of such expenditures without profit to the contractor, or they may, in their option, purchase the equipment, and expend any portion of said amount provided, at any point on the road where they may deem the same most advantageous to the company, whether on the section on which said reservation occurs or not.

Fourteenth. The telegraph line is included herein under the term "railroad," and is to be constructed in the same manner, and with similar materials, as in the lines east of the one hundredth meridian.

The said parties hereto, in consideration of the premises and of their covenants herein, do mutually agree, severally, to perform and fulfil their several respective agreements above written.

This contract having been submitted to the executive committee by resolution of the board of directors, August 16, 1867, and we having examined the details of the same, recommend its execution by the proper officers of the company with the Hon. Oakes Ames, the party named as the second part.

(Signed)

OLIVER AMES,
C. S. BUSHNELL,
SPRINGER HARBAUGH,
THOMAS C. DURANT,

Executive Committee Union Pacific Railroad Company.

This contract was adopted by the executive committee on October 1st, 1867, and one condition of its being adopted was that it should receive the written assent of all the stockholders of the Union Pacific Railroad Company. All this time the outstanding stock of the Railroad Company was continually increasing, and now amounted to about $5,000,000. This had been sold almost entirely among the stockholders of the Credit Mobilier, and of this, nearly, if not quite, eighty-five per cent. remained in the hands of such stockholders. But it was necessary that the control should be so absolutely in the hands of a few of the principal stockholders, that the management of the two concerns, until the completion of this immense contract, should not be changed. This was the next step to be settled, and it was settled beyond all controversy. It might become necessary before the completion of the contract, to place upon the market large amounts of the stock of the railroad company. This might pass into the hands of those hostile to the present directors; might, indeed, end in dissensions, and even jeopardize the successful completion of the road. Indeed, at the last election of directors previous to the making of this contract, the election was a very close one, and nearly resulted in a change of directors. The mighty responsibility that Mr. Ames had assumed in signing this contract, was too great to allow anything to stand between him and complete success. He had obligated himself, his heirs, executors, and administrators, for more than $47,000,000, perhaps the largest obligation ever assumed by a single individual in the United States, if not the world. Any error committed to defeat it, would ruin him for ever, and all those associated with him. Every point must be protected, every obstacle must be removed. The calculations had all been made; the initiatory steps had already been taken. Every avenue through which defeat could come had been guarded, and when the contract had been ratified by the stockholders, the machinery was all ready for operation. An assignment of this contract was made, not to the Credit Mobilier direct, but to certain trustees for the benefit of the stockholders of the Credit Mobilier, but not to *all*, but only such as being stockholders in the Union Pacific Railroad, should have made and executed powers of attorney or proxy, irrevocable, to said trustees, empowering them to vote upon at least six-tenths of all the shares of stock of the Union Pacific Railroad Company owned by said shareholders of the Credit Mobilier, and upon six-tenths of all that might come to them through any dividend resulting from said contract. This assignment is in the following words, viz. : —

ASSIGNMENT OF CONTRACT TO T. C. DURANT AND OTHERS.

MEMORANDUM of agreement, in triplicate, made this 15th day of October, 1867, between Oakes Ames, of North Easton, Massachusetts, party of the first part; Thomas C. Durant, of the City of New York, Oliver Ames, of North Easton, Massachusetts; John B. Alley, of Lynn, Massachusetts; Sidney Dillon, of the City of New York; Cornelius S. Bushnell, of New Haven, Connecticut; Henry S. McComb, of Wilmington, Delaware; Benjamin E. Bates, of Boston, Massachusetts, parties of the second part, and the Credit Mobilier, of America, party of the third part.

That, whereas the party of the first part has undertaken a certain large contract, for the construction of a certain portion, therein named, of the railroad and telegraph line of the Union Pacific Railroad Company, over the plains, and through and over the Rocky Mountains, which will require a very large and hazardous outlay of capital, which capital he is desirous to be assured of raising, at such times and in such sums as will enable him to complete and perform the said contract according to its terms and conditions; and

Whereas, the Credit Mobilier of America, the party of the third part, a corporation duly established by law, is empowered by its charter to advance and loan money in aid of such enterprises, and can control large amounts of capital for such purposes, and is willing to loan to said party of the first part such sums as may be found necessary to complete said contract, provided sufficient assurance may be made to said party of the third part therein, that said sums shall be duly expended in the work of completing said railroad and telegraph line, and that the payments for the faithful performance of said contract by said railroad company, shall be held and applied to reimburse said party of the third part for their loans and advances, together with a reasonable interest for the use of the money so loaned and advanced; and,

Whereas, said party of the third part fully believes that said contract, if honestly and faithfully executed, will be both profitable and advantageous to the parties performing the same, are therefore willing to guarantee the performance and execution of the same, for a reasonable commission to be paid therefor; and,

Whereas, both parties of the first and third part have confidence and reliance in the integrity, business capacity, and ability of the several persons named as parties of the second part hereto, and confidently believe that said persons have large interests, as well in the Union Pacific Railroad Company, as in the Credit Mobilier of America, they will execute and perform the said contract, and faithfully hold the proceeds thereof to the just use and benefit of the parties entitled thereto:

Therefore, it is agreed by and between the said parties of the first, second, and third part hereto, as follows, that is to say:

That said Oakes Ames, party of the first part hereto, hereby, for and in consideration of one dollar lawful money of the United States, to him duly paid by the party of the second part, and for divers other good and valuable considerations herein thereunto moving, doth hereby assign, set over, and transfer unto the said Thomas C. Durant, Oliver Ames, John B. Alley, Sidney Dillon, Cornelius S. Bushnell, Henry S. McComb, and Benjamin E. Bates, parties of the second part, all the right, title, and interest of, in, and to the said certain contract heretofore made and executed by and between the Union Pacific Railroad Company and the said Oakes Ames, bearing date the 16th day of August, 1867, for the construction of portions of the railroad and telegraph line of said railroad company, to which contract reference is herein made, for them, the said parties of the second part, to have and to hold the same to them and their survivors and successors forever in trust.

Nevertheless, upon the following trusts and conditions, and limitations, to wit:

First. That they, the said parties of the second part, shall perform all the terms and conditions of the said contract, so assigned, in all respects, which in and by the terms and conditions thereof, is undertaken and assumed and agreed to be done and performed by the said party of the first part herein named.

Second. That they, the said parties of the second part, shall hold all the avails and proceeds of the said contract, and therefrom shall reimburse themselves and the party of the third part hereto, all moneys advanced and expended by them, or either of them, in executing or performing the said contract, with interest and commission thereon, as hereinafter provided.

Third. Out of the said avails and proceeds, to pay unto the parties of the second part a reasonable sum as compensation for their services as such trustees for executing and performing the terms and conditions of this agreement, which compensation shall not exceed the sum of three thousand dollars per annum, to each and every one of the parties of the second part.

Fourth. To hold all the rest and residue of the said proceeds and avails for the use and benefit of such of the several persons holding and owning shares in the Capital stock of the said Credit Mobilier of America, on the day of the date hereof, in proportion to the number of shares which said stockholders now severally hold and own, and for the use and benefit of such of the several assignees and holders of such shares of stock at the times herein set forth, for the distribution of said residue and remainder of said avails and proceeds, who shall comply with the provisions, conditions, and limitations herein contained, which are, on their part, to be complied with.

Fifth. To pay over, on or before the first Wednesday of June and December in each year, or within thirty days thereafter, his just share and proportion of the residue and remainder of the said proceeds and avails as shall be justly estimated by the said trustees to have been made and earned as net profit on said contract, during the preceding six months, to each shareholder only in said Credit Mobilier of America, who, being a stockholder in the Union Pacific Railroad, shall have made and executed his power of attorney or proxy, irrevocable to said several parties of the second part, their survivors and successors, empowering them, the said parties of the second part, to vote upon at least six-tenths of all the shares of stock owned by said shareholders of the Credit Mobilier of America, in the capital stock of the Union Pacific Railroad Company, on the day of the date hereof, and six-tenths of any stock in said Union Pacific Railroad Company, he may have received as dividend or otherwise, because, or by virtue of having been a stockholder in said Credit Mobilier of America, or which may appertain to any shares in said Union Pacific Railroad Company, which had been so assigned to him at the time or times of the distribution of the said profits as herein provided ; and this trust is made and declared upon the express condition and limitation that it shall not inure in any manner or degree to the use or benefit of any stockholder of the Credit Mobilier of America, who shall neglect or refuse to execute and deliver unto the said parties of the second part his proxy or power of attorney, in the manner and for the purpose hereinbefore provided ; or who shall in any way, or by any proceeding, knowingly hinder, delay, or interfere with the execution or performance of the trust and conditions herein declared and set forth.

Then follow other conditions, that said trustees shall act with the majority of said trustees ; that all their votes should be recorded ; that an office should be kept in the city of New York ; meetings of said trustees to be called by the secretary ; that such secretary should be appointed by the trustees, and should keep the accounts and vouchers of all transactions, his books to be open to the inspection of any trustee ; that said trustees should cause a monthly statement, showing amount due from the railroad, to be made to the Credit Mobilier : also, in case of a vacancy in the board of trustees, the vacancy to be filled by remaining trustees; in case of wilful neglect or fraud of any trustee, he was to be deprived of his trusteeship, and all interest through or under the contract. The trustees agreed to accept the trust, and faithfully perform its conditions. The Credit Mobilier agreed to advance the necessary funds at seven per cent. interest, and to guarantee the performance and execution of the contract, and to hold harmless and indemnify the parties of the first and second part, from any loss through said contract, for a commission of two and one-half per cent. of the money advanced by it, and a further agreement that the net profits of the work finished on the first hundred miles prior to January 1, 1867, should be paid to the Credit Mobilier.

This assignment is signed by Oakes Ames, by each of the seven trustees, and by the Credit Mobilier of America by Sidney Dillon, president.

Such is the contract and its assignment; and in what respect does it differ from the contract of Hoxie, except in its magnitude and difference in the parties. The one was given to an irresponsible person, who, it was never intended, should complete the contract, but was used as a figure head to transfer the contract to the Credit Mobilier—in other words, back to the Pacific Railroad. And it is indeed understood and claimed by many, even of those who have paid the subject much attention, that the other, though a man of large means, of great executive ability, took the contract simply for the purpose

of turning it over to a board of trustees composed of
the officers and directors and principal stockholders
of the two corporations, who should then hold the
absolute control of both corporations, and who, by
this means, could use for their own exclusive benefit
the extraordinary franchises, and concessions, and
loans which the government had made to push
forward the building of the Pacific Railroad; but
this is a position which cannot be maintained by
any one who will give the subject a careful consideration, and try to arrive at a true understanding
of this contract and its assignment.

We are ready to affirm—and we believe this
contract and assignment will bear us out—that
the Credit Mobilier, as a corporation, had nothing
whatever to do with this contract or its execution.
We have before alluded to the hostility of Mr.
Durant toward the Credit Mobilier. No contract
could, by reason of that hostility, be made to the
Credit Mobilier, or to any one who would assign
it to that company. As matters were standing, the
construction of the road must soon be brought to an
end. The Credit Mobilier had indeed been constructing a part of the road without any contract,
but this was a dangerous proceeding, and might end
in total loss. Efforts were made to get some contractor to take a contract, but in all the country
there was no man so foolish. At last efforts for a
compromise were made, and rather than see the
road fail, rather than see that project, to which his
life was devoted, brought to an inglorious end,

Mr. Ames was prevailed upon to take the contract. In taking it his motives were high, honorable, and patriotic. The road was a public, a national necessity. To falter now, the consequences might be the abandonment for generations of any attempt to cross the continent by means of a railroad. Mr. Ames considered well the responsibility he assumed. He believed also that by proper management the road could be built at the contract price, so that a small profit could be realized to the contractor, and he firmly believed that when the road was once completed the increase of business along its line would make its securities valuable. There was one condition he imposed, and that was that the contract must receive the assent of every stockholder of the Union Pacific Railroad, in writing When the question was raised as to the manner in which this mighty contract was to be executed, Mr. Ames insisted that he must take the contract untrammeled by any promise, agreement, or understanding. He could tell no man what he would do. "Of course," said Mr. Ames, "I must have associates, but no man shall be wronged, no one shall be deprived of his rights. I am an honest man, and I will see that every man is protected."

V.

THE ASSIGNMENT TO SEVEN TRUS-
TEES.

BOTH sides to the controversy which made this contract necessary, placed the utmost confidence in Mr. Ames, and in the integrity of his character, and were sure that the rights of all would be protected. Thus Mr. Ames took this great contract, with no agreement, understanding, or promise. He made none, and none was exacted of him. Yet all felt a confidence in him that the contract would be so used that the interests of all should be guarded. The contract properly belonged to the Credit Mobilier, which had commenced the construction of the road, and had continued it up to the date of the contract. Its entire capital had been absorbed in that work, and not one cent of returns had been made to the stockholders. What profit there was, if any had been made, had been misappropriated by those who had formerly held the management. $3,750,000, which those stockholders had paid for the capital stock of that company, were now in the Union Pacific roadbed. That road had reaped the benefit, while the men who paid the money had nothing to show for it. This was the view which Mr. Ames took, and he determined that this contract should inure to their benefit—to them as individuals and not as a corporation. He therefore made his assignment to seven trustees for their benefit, provided they would share with him the responsibility of the contract; and provided also that they were holders of Union Pacific stock. It was an assignment for the benefit of certain specified individuals, those individuals being also stockholders in the Credit Mobilier. This term was used to designate them, because of its simplicity, and had no relation to the corporation of which they were members. If, instead of the fourth and fifth clauses of the declaration of trust contained in the assignment above, the wording had been "To hold all the rest and residue of the said proceeds and avails for the use and benefit of (here naming each individual stockholder of the Credit Mobilier by name), in the proportion following, to wit, to (here designate the proportion which each was to have, it being the same proportion as the stock owned by him bore to the entire capital stock of the Credit Mobilier, &c.") By doing this the exact object desired would have been obtained, and the connection with the Credit Mobilier—unfortunate as it proved to be—would have been avoided. Then could have followed the condition about giving proxies, and everything would have been precisely as it was, without the complications that afterwards arose. At this time there were about one hundred stockholders in the Credit Mobilier, and so for convenience the designation of " stockholders in the Credit Mobilier " was used.

Upon these grounds it is that we affirm that the
Credit Mobilier had nothing whatever to do with the
Ames contract. This position has also been affirmed
by the Supreme Court of Pennsylvania, where the
Credit Mobilier was sued for taxes to the amount of
$1,200,000, upon the dividends declared by the
trustees, and it was there decided that the Credit
Mobilier had declared no dividends. Could stronger
arguments be used than that the State of Pennsylvania decided against its own claim to the amount
of more than a million dollars?

Upon this assignment being made, the Union
Pacific Railroad Company released Mr. Oakes
Ames from any personal liability under the contract he had signed. The great liability which
Mr. Ames assumed, in less than two months had
entirely vanished, and again he was as free as before
he signed it. Under that contract he incurred no
liability; he did not even enter upon the fulfilling of
the contract, but for these two months it lay dormant;
in fact, for nearly this entire time it was inoperative.
It needed the written assent of all the stockholders
of the Union Pacific Railroad, and this assent was
not obtained until after the first of October. So that
in fact and in reality, the personal liability of Oakes
Ames under the contract amounted to nothing.
There was, however, a difference in one respect
which should be noticed, and which, indeed, has a
very powerful bearing upon not only the liability of
Oakes Ames, but of every beneficiary under the
contract. One condition which Mr. Oakes Ames

insisted upon before he would accept the contract was, that it should receive the assent in writing of every stockholder of the Union Pacific Railroad. This was obtained. He then assigned the contract to the trustees, and then the agreement which all the stockholders in both companies made, made them each individually liable under that contract. Though Oakes Ames was in reality released from personal liability under the contract by the Union Pacific Railroad Company, upon his assigning the contract, he, in common with all others, again took that liability upon himself, and no man bore the brunt of that liability more than did he. His whole immense fortune was involved in the undertaking; and it came near wrecking him financially. He was at one time forced, by reason of the responsibility under this contract, and his investments therein, to suspend payment in his regular business, and ask for an extension by his creditors. His liabilities at that time amounted to some $8,000,000. But, with a courage seldom, if ever equalled, he continued on in this enterprise, and at last was successful, and saw the road completed. In time all his creditors were fully satisfied.

From this time forth the control of the Union Pacific Railroad passed from the hands of its directors and officers, into the hands of the seven trustees who were constructing the road, and into their hands, irrevocable powers of attorney had been given by the stockholders to vote upon their shares, thus enabling them to hold absolute control so long as they should desire. Certainly they were not long in understanding the position in which they were now placed. In fact, had they not long worked for this? Had they not, by means of the influence of the name of Oakes Ames among the stockholders, obtained it? The very day following the assignment, these trustees entered into an agreement among themselves whereby they bound themselves to vote not only with their own shares, but with the proxies held by them for such directors of the Union Pacific Railroad as should be nominated by a majority of the then existing board of directors, not appointed by the president, and no others; and, in case of a failure to nominate by such directors, then to vote for the elected members of the existing board, and, in case any of said trustees should refuse to stand by this agreement, he was to forfeit all claims for benefits or dividends under the contracts assigned to them.

Though Mr. Oakes Ames had assigned his entire contract; though thereafter he had no more to do with the contract than any other stockholder of the Union Pacific Railroad Company; though he had no special authority, he was not without interest by any means, for he was one of the largest stockholders in each corporation, and upon its success depended its profits. His liability as a contractor had ceased (though immediately assumed in another form), yet his influence was in a great measure necessary for the successful completion of the contract. Under this contract no work had been done prior to its assignment to the trustees, yet work had been progressing, and the road was being pushed forward rapidly by the Credit Mobilier; and at the date of the assignment—which is essentially the date of the ratification of the contract by the stockholders—there had been 238 miles of the road completed, which were embraced in this contract—in other words, more than one-third of the whole contract was completed before a stroke had been done. Yet these 238 miles, which had been completed at a cost not exceeding $27,500 per mile (including equipment) to the company, were paid for to the trustees at a rate of over $42,000 per mile. This was a profit—if such a name is applicable to it—of between $2,500,000 and $3,000,000 under this contract for which no work was needed or ever done, though all this work had been done by the Credit Mobiler, or more strictly speaking, by the stockholders of the Credit Mobiler.

In less than two months after the assignment (viz., December 12, 1867,) the first dividend was declared, which was $2,244,000 in first mortgage bonds of the Union Pacific Railroad Company, and $2,244,000 in the stock of the company. Considering the bonds at that time worth eighty-five cents, and the stock thirty cents on the dollar, would make the actual cash value of that dividend at the time it was declared, about $2,580,600; and this, beyond all question, is the extra compensation paid to these trustees on account of the road already completed, and to that extent a payment to the stockholders of the Credit Mobiler for the work done by them without a contract. From this amount there should be deducted $1,104,000 paid by the trustees to the Credit Mobilier on account of the road included in this contract, which had been constructed by that Company. These trustees continued to work under this Ames contract until it was completed. The work was pushed forward with wonderful rapidity, and as a natural consequence greatly increased the cost of construction. It was asserted by one of the trustees that had the full time been taken in which to complete the road, it could have been built at scarcely more than one-half what it did cost.

Great stress has been laid on the fact that at the time the Ames contract was made, the estimated cost of building the road over the mountains was greatly in excess of what it really cost on account of the discovery of a new route which was much more easy and far less expensive. This is set forth as one excuse why the Ames contract was to include all from the 100th meridian; that by so doing the contract would be less for the whole distance, and thus the average expense would be the same, for there being a large profit upon the first portion, the contractor could afford to take a less sum per mile for the more difficult portion. But it is a fact well settled that the very route upon which the road was built was known months before that contract was given, and the advantages of that route were all known to the contractor, and were considered by him in his calculations, and in making these calculations no one believed that the more difficult portions of the road could be built for the price named in the contract, and had not this portion been included, the average for the balance must have been necessarily largely increased. But there remains the other fact, which should not be forgotten, that the completed work included in this contract had been performed by the Credit Mobilier; and by the contract and its assignment, the trustees were to repay the Credit Mobilier for this work, which was done, and out of the money so received the Credit Mobilier declared the only dividend it ever made.

It is claimed that the plan of letting this contract to Mr. Ames, including as it did the finished portion, ignored the right of the government in the premises, and was calculated to destroy all that interest. The government had given them the right of way, had granted them large subsidies of money for every mile of road to be built, and had consented to take a second mortgage as security; had given them the privilege of creating a debt equal to the amount advanced by the government, which should have precedence; and in return asked that a certain proportion of the net profits should go to the government, and that the government should have the right to regulate the fares when the net profits should exceed a certain per cent. on the cost of the road, and that by this vast increase in the cost of the road the interest of the government was practically destroyed, and the claim to regulate tariffs made of no effect. But we shall have occasion to consider this right of the government further on.

The Ames contract was finished, but in the meantime another contract had been let and, in a few days after it was made, was assigned to these same trustees. This, the Davis contract, was for the balance of the road, from the end of the Ames contract, and embraced about $125\frac{23}{100}$ miles, and it was upon the same terms and conditions as the Ames contract. Under these three contracts was constructed the entire road.

The difficulties which were surmounted were such as to attract the attention of the world. It was the greatest enterprise ever undertaken in America. It was the first, and public opinion must be controlled,— public confidence must be secured; the capitalists of the country must be induced to put their money into an enterprise where failure was openly predicted and by the many firmly believed; there was no security except the obligation of the seven trustees, and the bonds of the government, which then were below par. It was a question open to discussion whether the road would pay even if completed. The debt that must be created was large, and seemingly impossible to meet; the rate of interest was great, and would eat up all the earnings of the road. The operating expenses must necessarily be large. The local business of the road could not be depended upon for any considerable income, until the country through which it passed should become settled, and that country was then believed to be but little better than a desert, where nothing but the hardy sage-bush would grow, or else it was through the mountains, where even man could not live. Indeed the undertaking was a hazardous one; indeed it was enough to appall the stoutest heart, and to frighten the most reckless capitalist. Yet these men were not to be diverted from their course; they had embarked their names, their fortunes upon its accomplishment, and the most discouraging events could not make them abandon the object of their lives.

Though they were, many of them, men of immense resources, though their credit had stood in business circles the very highest, they soon found their credit in many places badly shaken, and their ability to carry on the mighty work greatly impeded. They were compelled to take the securities of the road and to hold them, because no market could be found for them; they were forced to borrow money at most ruinous rates of interest; they were forced to place the bonds of the road in pledge for the necessary capital, and that at times at the rate of three dollars to one. It needed the most watchful care, the greatest ability in the country, and the most extraordinary energy to carry it on, and all this it had. In spite of all discouragements the road was completed — completed seven years before the time limited — and it became at once a national highway; the country through which it passed was found to be, a fair proportion of the distance, the nearest approach to the Garden of Eden now found on earth. Towns and cities sprang up along the line. Territories became states, and a happy, prosperous people swarmed over those once desolate plains to find there homes of contentment and peace. Business was greatly increased, far beyond even the expectation of its builders; but there was yet much to do.

Much capital was needed, and it was necessary that the men who had risked their all in its completion should now stand ready to aid it still with their means. Even with the success already attained, had the support of these men been removed, the road would have become bankrupt, and the millions that had been spent in its construction would have been wasted. At the completion of the road the company found itself $6,000,000 in debt, and this burden must fall upon individuals, to be followed by others necessary to keep the road in active operation until a business was created affording revenue sufficient to meet the running expenses and interest, and this burden was sufficient to destroy nearly all profit derived from the building of the road.

What was that profit? Was it so great as to alarm any thinking mind? Was it such as to call forth the criticism of the public? Was it such as to convince the world that great corruption had been used to secure it? In estimating profit, we should always consider the outlay, and the risk assumed. In considering this portion of the subject, the figures will be taken mostly from the testimony brought out by the Congressional committee of investigation, in 1873. From the report of the committee it appears that

THE COST TO THE RAILROAD COMPANY OF

The Hoxie contract was - - - - $12,974,416 24
    Ames contract - - - - - 57,140,102 94
    Davis contract - - - - - 23,431,768 10

Making total cost - - - - - $93,546,287 28

THE COST TO THE CONTRACTORS OF

The Hoxie contract $ 7,806,183 33
    Ames contract   27,285,141 99
    Davis contract   15,629,633 62   50,720,958 94

Leaving a profit to contractors - $42,825,328 34
In addition to this, there was a payment to the Credit Mobilier on account of fifty-eight miles, - - -   1,104,000 00

Making the total profit - - - - $43,929,328 34

This profit, it should be remembered, includes the payments of bonds and stock at par, and not at its cash value. It is therefore necessary to ascertain the proportionate value of each of this class of payments in order to ascertain what was the *cash* profit in the construction of the road. The books of the company show that the profits under the Ames and Davis contracts were composed of

$3,777,000 first mortgage bonds, worth ninety cents on the dollar.

$4,400,000 certificates for first mortgage bonds, afterwards converted into income bonds at above par.

$5,841,000 income bonds, at sixty.
$24,000,000 stock of Union Pacific Railroad Co.
$2,346,195 cash.

The stock of the Union Pacific Railroad, as has been stated above, was worth about thirty cents on the dollar. Sometimes the price would advance and sometimes would fall, but for all their calculations the average price was thirty cents.

Upon this basis the actual cash profits of the Ames and Davis contracts would be as follows:

$3,777,000 first mortgage bonds at ninety	$3,399,300 00
$4,400,000 certificates for first mortgage bonds	4,425,000 00
$5,841,000 income bonds at sixty	3,504,000 00
$24,000,000 stock at thirty	7,200,000 00
$2,346,195 cash	2,346,195 00
Making a total cash profit	$20,874,495 00

The profits on the Hoxie contract consisted of $1,125,000 first mortgage bonds at eighty-five, and $5,147,232 71 stock at thirty, and making the same reduction as above, we have —

$1,125,000 bonds at eighty-five	$956,250 00
$5,147,232 71 stock at thirty	1,544,169 81
As the cash profit of the Hoxie cont'ct	2,500,419 81
And if to this is added the profits as above	20,874,495 00
Making total profit of the whole road	23,374,914 81

In this connection attention is called to the aid which the government extended to the road, in its own bonds, and in the first mortgage bonds which the government had allowed the road to issue and to make a lien upon the road prior to the claim of the government.

First mortgage bonds issued	$27,213,000 00
Sold at a discount of	3,494,991 23
Net proceeds	$23,718,008 77
Government bonds issued	$27,236,512 00
Sold at a discount of	91,348 72
Net proceeds	$27,145,163 28
The net proceeds of the two classes of bonds	$50,863,172 05
We have seen that the actual cost of the whole road to the contractors was	50,720,958 94
Value of the bonds over cost of construction	142,213 11

In other words, the net proceeds of the government and first mortgage bonds were sufficient to pay for the construction of the entire road, and from the stock, the income bonds, and land grant bonds, the contractors received in cash value at last $23,000,000 as profit, being about forty-eight per cent. of the whole cost. This profit, which certainly is a large one in whatever light it may be considered, it is claimed by the directors of the Credit Mobilier is not the correct statement of the case, but that the actual profit received by them is far less than this — that it did not, in fact, aggregate more than about fifteen per cent.; but how any such conclusion can be reached from the figures presented by the *committee* is far more than the ordinary intellect can understand. The claim is made, and with some force, that at times the stock which they took was worth far less than thirty, and that sales were made even as low as nine cents on the dollar; but even considering that the entire issue had been sold at that rate the cash profit would have reached at least $16,000,000, or about thirty-two per cent. on the cost. But the evidence of all parties was that the average net price of the stock was thirty cents on the dollar.

This is the reasoning of the committee on investigation in Congress, but it seems to us as a most wilful perversion of figures, — an unauthorized use of those figures to prove a proposition which had been in their minds at the start, and which they were determined to maintain and prove, it mattered not by what means. This estimate made by the committee leaves out from the cost of the road a large number of items, which were expenditures of the Credit Mobilier, but which might not enter into an estimate of the "actual cost" of building the road. Every man who has done any business knows full well that there are always expenses that could not be calculated as items of this "actual cost." Such was, indeed, the testimony of the witnesses before this committee, but that testimony was utterly ignored by the committee in their report. It would tell against their argument, and the bias which it is manifest they entertained from the beginning of the investigation. Again, the committee refused to take notice of the testimony of losses, amounting to millions of dollars, which the Credit Mobilier sustained, notably the loss of their entire capital of $3,750,000, which had been paid in in cash, and was entirely used up in the construction of the road, and which should properly be deducted from the profits shown. The committee also have recorded as profits the transfer of money from one account to another; as an instance, the payment by the trustees of $1,104,000 to the Credit Mobilier. The committee cite it as a payment by the Union Pacific Railroad Company. Again, the committee have figured as *profits* actual *losses*, as may be seen in the bonus which the Credit Mobilier was compelled to give in order to get the additional capital subscribed for. As an inducement to the sale of these additional shares, the Credit Mobilier gave $1,000 in first mortgage bonds for each $1,000 subscription to the stock. In this way $1,125,000 of these bonds were disposed of, it being a loss to the company of that amount, but which the committee have set forth as a profit. Nor have the committee noticed the great losses which the Credit Mobilier and the trustees sustained in their endeavors to find a market for the securities they had taken. It was clearly in evidence that more than $5,000,000 of Union Pacific stock was sold by the Credit Mobilier at $4.50 per share, because it could be disposed of in no other way.

But now the actual profit earned by the Credit Mobilier and the trustees was in evidence before the committee, but in their report they made no allusion to it; let us do that, and then we may understand. There was never any question raised but that all the profits made under these contracts were divided. In fact, the committee states that such was thè case. Below will be found the date of each dividend, the amount and the cash value of each, reckoning the bonds at 85 and the stock at 30 :—

Dec. 12, 1867,	$2,543,208	First mortgage bonds,	$2,161,726	80
Dec. 12, 1867,	2,543,208	Union Pacific Stock, - -	726,962	40
Jan. 3, 1868,	748,000	First mortgage bonds, -	635,800	00
June 17, 1868,	2,201,204	Cash, - - - - - - -	2,201,204	00
July 8, 1868,	1,112,768	Cash, - - - - - - -	1,112,768	00
July 3, 1868,	2,804,050	First mortgage bonds, -	2,383,442	50
Dec. 29, 1868,	7,500,000	Union Pacific Stock, - -	2,250,000	00
Dec., 1867,	420,000	12 per cent. div. Cr. Mob.,	420,000	00
	19,872,438		11,891,903	70
Deducting the loss of the Credit Mobilier capital, (which was an entire loss), - - - - - - - -			3,750,000	00
Leaves as the net profits, cash value, - - - - -			8,141,903	70

To this there should, perhaps, be added the present value of the Credit Mobilier stock. But that value is uncertain, and if the utmost that is claimed by some should be realized, there might be added about $2,000,000 to this as the total profits. But these claims are very uncertain.

This being all the profit realized from an expenditure of about $70,000,000 or about 12 per cent. But not counting at all this loss of capital, the profit would be but little over 16 per. cent. upon the cost. This conclusion coincides with all the testimony before the committee, and to an unprejudiced mind shows the bias of this committee, and the determination to unearth some gigantic fraud, whether it existed there or not. From this report were derived nearly all the arguments that were made before Congress upon this subject, and which arguments have tended to so large an extent to influence the public mind, and prejudice the public against the operations of the Credit Mobilier. But how changed is the result! The immense profits of $43,000,000 which have been paraded before the country, have dwindled down to less than ten millions, upon an expenditure of some $70,000,000. Certainly this is a profit that may of itself sound large, but it was the result of some four years work, and of great expenditure. The profit was not larger than that which some of our merchant princes were making at the same time and against whom no thought of wrong was ever entertained, but whose industry and skill were highly commended.

VI.

THE DIFFICULTIES OF CONSTRUCTION.

WE must at all times consider the risk, and the circumstances under which that risk was taken. It should be remembered that there was no one else willing to undertake so great a contract, no one who would be willing to risk all he had in such an endeavor. He must feel sure that he could recover himself from his great outlay, and this no one could do. The company had tried to build the road itself and had wholly failed, so that it became necessary to even sell their rolling stock to pay their debts. Whatever was done must be done under the greatest disadvantage. All materials used in construction had to be transported overland or by means of the Missouri River, which was exceedingly expensive. The people were afraid it would not succeed, and at times could not be induced to buy its bonds, and thus indeed the capital necessary for its completion could not be obtained. Under all these discouraging circumstances this construction company took hold of the work and pushed it forward to completion. Why was a construction company necessary? It was necessary in order to limit the liability in case of loss. Individuals engaging in it might find themselves involved as partners to the full extent of all debts contracted, while the liability of the construction company was limited to the amount of its capital. But this was only one reason. There were others more powerful. By the charter under which the road was built, it was provided that the capital stock was to be $100,000,000, and that the books for subscriptions to stock were to remain open until the whole amount should be subscribed. To have enabled any company or set of men to obtain control of the road would have rendered necessary a subscription of some $51,000,000. Such a subscription was an utter impossibility. Every effort that could be made was made at the beginning, and in two years the total subscriptions amounted to only a trifle over $2,000,000. No man or company could be induced to engage in such a gigantic scheme unless they could be assured that, when the work was in progress, and success assured, they were to remain secure in their hope of profit. Supposing that a subscription of $36,000,000 (the amount of stock finally issued,) had been made, and the work gone on. Here there would have been no chance for any profit to be made from construction, for the work would then be done by the road itself, and the only chance for any profit from this investment would be in the running of the road after its completion. When the work was so far along that its successful completion was assured, another party of capitalists might come forward, and by new subscriptions, for the books must still remain open, could obtain control of the road, while those who had built the road, who had borne all the risk of the enterprise, who had staked their money on the work, who had risked their fortunes on its construction, would be deprived of all voice in the management or control of the road, by those who had borne no risk at all. It was this fact that rendered it impossible to obtain subscriptions, and build the road as the charter suggested. By means of the construction company, all these dangers were avoided. Under no other conditions could the road have been built at all, and under this plan every right of the government was amply protected, and the interests of every stockholder fully secured.

The greatest point that is made against this proceeding is that the construction company, as organized, consisted of the same men who directed the other company with whom they contracted. While this may have been, under most circumstances in which the government was interested, against policy and good faith, there was certainly no law forbidding it — there was no question as to its technical legality; and it is a serious question whether a better contract could have been made by or with any other company, though wholly separate and distinct in interest from the other. None save those who were intimately interested in the success of the road, could be induced to touch such a contract. It was not as though other roads had reached across the continent, demonstrating beyond a doubt that such an enterprise was possible of success; it was not as though the certainty of its accomplishment had inspired the confidence of the public in it, and had made it plain that it would be safe for capital to invest. Like all first experiments, it had all these obstacles to overcome and subdue. It was like the pioneer who goes far into the wilderness to prepare a foothold for the more timid to follow. The success of the first endeavor has made it easy to inspire public confidence in other similar endeavors, and now in the popularity of such undertakings we are apt to lose sight of the circumstances surrounding the first. The first was completed, and has been in successful operation for more than eleven years, but to this day, though various lines have been started, and have received the same fostering care and assistance of the government, not one in this length of time has opened a line to the Pacific, and will not for some years to come. They certainly do not have so great difficulties to surmount. Public confidence has been established, and it has been demonstrated that such roads can be built, and that when built, are, or can be made, paying investments. However great may be the cry against the immense profits that the Credit Mobilier made in the construction of the Union Pacific Railroad, all this cry has arisen out of the fact that certain members of Congress became interested in the stock of the Credit Mobilier, and political capital was made out of it for the purpose of controlling elections. Other roads have been built in the same way, and are still being built in the same manner. How many people are there now to whom the name of Credit Mobilier is perfectly familiar, who have ever heard of the Contract and Finance Company ? and who, if asked to-day, could tell when or where such an organization ever existed ? And yet it is a corporation almost identical with the Credit Mobilier, so far as its purposes and organization are concerned, and in the work which it did. The Contract and Finance Company was organized under the laws of the State of California, and was used for the purpose of constructing the Central Pacific Railroad from San Francisco to its junction with the Union Pacific Railroad. It was in operation at the same time that the Credit· Mobilier was at work on the eastern side of the Rocky Mountains, and was composed of the principal stockholders of the Central Pacific Railroad. This company had a contract to build some six hundred miles of the road, and the profits that arose from that construction were very large—far larger than those of the Credit Mobilier—and this profit, instead of being divided among the stockholders of the Central Pacific Railroad, as were the profits of the Credit Mobilier among the stockholders of the Union Pacific Railroad, went into the pockets of a very few individuals. In effect these few individuals took the contract of building the road, of themselves as representatives for that road, at an immense profit. The government was interested in the road the same, and to the same extent, as in the Union Pacific Railroad. But how changed the circumstances when a few members of Congress happened to own a few shares in the one. The one has been condemned unmercifully*; its officers, and those interested in it, have been branded as felons; its name has become a by-word for infamy, while the other, pursuing the same plan, only not half so liberal to the general public, has gone free, and its name, even, is almost unheard of outside of special circles. Was the government defrauded by the one? then also was it by the other. Was its principle wrong? then so was that of the other. Is the one to be condemned? then so must the other. Must a policy of hate be inaugurated against the one? then so must it against the other. Must the one be held up for public condemnation? then so must the other. They meet alike on common ground. They were each actuated by the same motives. The public has received the same great and wonderful advantages from each. A great national highway has been constructed. The union of our common country has been cemented by ties that can never be broken; and even though the loans made by the government should never be paid, already has the government saved enough to more than repay all the outlay.

Whether all this has been the result of the labors of the Credit Mobilier it is hard to say, and certainly as hard to deny. The interests of the Union Pacific Railroad and the Credit Mobilier are so interwoven with each other that it is impossible to separate them. Certain it is that, without the intervention of a construction company, the Union Pacific Railroad would never have been built. But whether it was absolutely necessary that that construction company should be identical with the Railroad Company, is the only question that can be raised against the plan of its operations. It is claimed that this combination was against equity and good conscience, and that the directors of the Union Pacific Railroad Company had no right to make a contract with themselves, though under the guise of another corporation, by which they would make for themselves a profit from the funds of the Railroad Company; but that they must, even in that capacity, be regarded as trustees for the Railroad, and whatever profit was made through their contract must inure to the benefit of the Railroad. While this may all be true, the question would naturally arise, for whom, in that capacity, would they become trustees? The answer must be, for the holders of the stock of the Union Pacific Railroad. What was the nature of the agreement by which they held their trust? It was that all the profits arising from the contract should be paid to the holders of the stock of the Credit Mobilier, and those stockholders were identically the same as the holders of the stock of the Union Pacific Railroad. It was clearly in evidence that such was the case, and where there were any who would not sign the agreement giving to the trustees their irrevocable power of attorney or proxy to vote on their shares, their stock was bought as far as it was possible, so that no stock should be unrepresented in the division of profits. It should also be remembered that every stockholder agreed in writing to the Ames and Davis contracts, and thus certainly no advantage was taken of their position. Was the government a party who should have been consulted? What was the interest of the government? The government gave the right of way on the condition that the road should be built; it gave on the same condition large subsidies of land. It also loaned the road a certain amount of its bonds, consenting that its claim should be a second lien on the road, subject to an equal indebtedness, to be created by the Railroad Company, those bonds to be paid by the Railroad at the expiration of thirty years; and, in case of the net profits of the road exceeding ten per cent. of the cost of the road, the government to have the right to regulate the rates of fare, and reserved to itself the right to appoint certain directors of the road, and the right to legislate upon the charter as granted. Have any of the conditions which the government required been unfulfilled? The road was completed as required, a first-class road, and was completed some seven years before it was required. Upon the completion of the road the grants of land and right of way became absolutely the property of the road, and the government had no cause to complain. In fact, the government became, by the early completion of the road, a great gainer, and saved, by that event alone, millions of dollars every year. Was the cost of the road greatly increased by the manner in which it was built? and by that means were the future claims of the government rendered of no account? Was it the duty of the company to build the road by using as little of the loan of the government as possible, or had the road the right to use all of the loan which the government granted? And if the company, in building the road, let the contracts to themselves, did they thereby stand in such a relation to the government that they must account for all the profits they received? If any question should arise as to the accounting to the shareholders of the Union Pacific stock, those questions are fully answered in the fact that an equal division of all profits was made with the holders of that stock; they not only all agreed to the contracts and arrangements, but themselves received whatever profit arose from the execution of those contracts. But could the road have been built at a less price than it was? Suppose that the $36,000,000 represented by the stock, had been paid into the treasury in cash, it is even probable that, under such circumstances, the road could not have been built at all. Economy and frugality, under such circumstances, could not have been expected. The country at large, seeing that the work was sure to go through, urged, in every way possible, the utmost speed of construction ; and more, Congress had given to the Central Pacific Railroad Company the right to build its road until it should meet the Union Pacific, and thus set the two great companies on a race across the continent. At this time there was no road across the State of Iowa, and all the materials must be transported overland, or by way of the Missouri River, from Saint Louis to Omaha, at immense cost. At the commencement of the building of the road no satisfactory route had been selected across the mountains. It was building a railroad across a country without timber, without fuel, without water, (all of which must be transported), with gold at 160 and iron $160 per ton, with gangs of men at work both day and night, with half the force engaged in keeping the Indians from killing the other half; and all these working together would have created a spirit of extravagance that would have wasted the entire capital of the company, and left the road unfinished. As these men undertook the enterprise, it seemed to those careful capitalists of the country a wild waste of money, in the most favorable light. There was a spirit of adventure about it, of loyalty and courage, such as were never before seen in the history of railroad enterprise. The conditions were utterly inconsistent with anything like prudence or economy. Had all that money been in the treasury, the road would necessarily have been built by day's work, for no responsible contractor could have been found to take a contract when he had to freight his materials at such vast expense, and where he had to keep a standing army to protect his workmen from the Indians; and it has been asserted by those well qualified to judge, that the contract assumed by Mr. Ames was the wildest contract ever made by a civilized man.

In taking this contract as they did, these men were forced to exercise as great economy as possible in order to realize any profit at all, and the costs, outside of what appears as the actual cost of construction, were enormous; and beyond all, it is a fact that even with as much economy as could have been used, all the money invested in the enterprise would have been wasted except for the accidental discovery of coal along the route. At the time the road commenced operations they were paying from nineteen dollars to twenty dollars per cord for wood that was not the equivalent of more than one third or one fourth of a ton of coal. The cost of the road, then, as it was built by the Credit Mobilier, is less than would have been the cost could it have been possible to have built the road otherwise. The intervention of the construction company was necessary. The interest which the stockholders had in the success of the railroad is all that made it possible for the road to be built. The government has not been wronged. Every obligation which the road was to perform has been performed. The government paid no money; it merely lent its credit, and its relation to the road is that of a creditor to a debtor with a lien. The government can not be in the slightest injured if the debt is paid. But it is said the debt has not been paid; but it is not due, and the government, the same as an individual, has no right to collect a debt before it is due. The security which the government took is that of its own choosing. It ought not to complain of that, and the only right which the government might assume is to prevent the waste of its mortgage security, so that the debt may be paid when due. This right the government has assumed, and a sinking fund has been established, by means of which every dollar of the bonds advanced by the government will be paid at its maturity. Into this sinking fund the Railroad Company is yearly turning a large amount of money. But yet the Railroad Company has really *paid* no money into this sinking fund. The amount due the company from the government on half transportation account has been sufficient to meet any such requirement, without the payment by the company of a dollar from its other earnings. How can the government be wronged by any such showing as that?

The government has everything that it required of the road, and has assurance that every dollar will be repaid. The government has never parted with a dollar, except interest that it has paid on the bonds, and its security is ample. It has, by this operation, secured advantages of unlimited value. The road has been the means of saving it millions of dollars every year, and has increased the value of its own land through which the road passes, to twice the former value, and has rendered it possible for that land to find a market, where before none existed at any price; and then, above all, the inestimable value the road has been to the whole country can never be understood. The internal commerce that has been created by it is far larger than the most enthusiastic advocate of the road had ever dreamed of.

In every respect the government has been the gainer, and in no respect has it been injured, or can it be injured.

If, then, there has been any wrong done in dividing the dividends among the stockholders of the Credit Mobilier, and that money is to be recovered, to whom would it belong? The answer must be, to the stockholders of the Union Pacific Railroad Company. But they are the very ones to whom it was divided, the stockholders of the Credit Mobilier and the Union Pacific Railroad being identical. We need not dwell upon this longer, for it is impossible to see how any wrong has been done any one. In fact none has been done.

In concluding this portion of our subject we desire to allude to one fact in relation to the different parties connected with the Credit Mobilier in the construction of this road, and the views which were held by them.

There were two parties in what has been familiarly known as the Union Pacfic Railroad ring, Durant and his friends constituting one and Oakes Ames and his associates the other. Their objects were as opposite as it was possible to be, and upon the prevailing of one or the other depended the success or utter failure of the road. The Durant party worked with the idea of building the road in the cheapest manner possible, for the purpose of making the largest profit conceivable from the contracts for construction, avowing that the road, when built, could never be a paying investment, and that those who looked for any profit in this line were deluded. They cared not how the road was constructed, so that it would be accepted by the government, and the government aid secured. They cared not to retain the stock of the company, and while this party was in the ascendency in the control of the Credit Mobilier, a large proportion of the stock taken in payment for constrnction was sold for four and one-half cents on the dollar. It was not considered by them of any value, for they were convinced that the road would never yield any returns to the stockholders. Not only was this done, but in their attempt to get the road accepted as they completed it, they paid to one government director $25,000 to induce him to report in favor of its acceptance.

The object of the Ames party was to build as good a road as possible, and have it fully completed and equipped. They did not have any expectation of receiving large profits from their contracts. It was their object to have a good road, and in its management, after completion, realize their profits. They believed that the business of the road would, in time, be large, and would yield large returns above running expenses. They had great hopes of the country through which the road was built, and believed that in a few years the local traffic would be immense. With this view in mind they retained as much of the stock of the road—which they took in payment for their work—as they could. Upon this they staked all their expectation of profit. The controlling minds in this policy were Oakes and Oliver Ames, and to their influence is due the successful building of the road.

A decade has shown the wisdom of their faith. The Union Pacific Railroad is now paying all its running expenses, all its interest, is making ample provision, in sinking funds, for the extinguishment of the government loan at its maturity, and is paying about eight per cent. dividends upon its stock, which has ready sale in open market at nearly par.

This result has been achieved by the faith and honesty of the Ameses, whose influence was strong enough to control the management of the construction company through whose instrumentality the road was built.

VII.

THE DISAGREEMENT WITH MR. McCOMB.

IN the former part of this work we have attempted to show the connection of the Credit Mobilier of America with the building of the Union Pacific Railroad, and in so doing we have found it necessary to go into some detail regarding the history of that road, the cost of its construction, &c., as all these matters necessarily came into a consideration of the workings and purposes of the Credit Mobilier. The two organizations were composed of the same persons and their interests became, in a great measure, identical, and it was impossible to separate them and to study them, except in connection one with the other. To the Credit Mobilier may justly belong the credit of building the Union Pacific Railroad, though it is true that to a great extent that organization did not in fact have the control, but upon its stockholders rested the responsibility, and to them came what profit there was in its construction. The great work that was accomplished will ever stand as the noblest monument of the achievements of mankind, and the blessings that have come upon the country through which it was built, by reason of its construction, can never be told, while coming generations will ever praise those through whose instrumentality it was built.

It is not natural that works of this character should ever assume the prominence that has been accorded the Credit Mobilier, unless some circumstance foreign to its main object should be associated with it. Such indeed was the case of the Credit Mobilier, and it is that circumstance which it shall be our purpose at this time to set forth. But for the accidental connection with it of certain members of Congress, its fame would never have extended beyond the knowledge of its own stockholders. It mattered not whether any crime was ever connected with it; it mattered not how pure may have been the motives of those who bought or sold that stock; it mattered not how large or small may have been the profits realized by the holders of that stock; it mattered not whether the government was the loser or gainer in its working; it was sufficient to know that political capital could be made out of it, and that some who held high places of trust and honor could be brought low, and their names forever clouded with infamy. Quietly the work had been done, an approving people had praised, and justly praised, the remarkable energy which had characterized those under whose management the work was done, and when that work was completed, millions joined in the glad shouts of rejoicing. Yet ere the last rail was laid, ere the last spike was driven, that riveted forever the band of union between the East and the West, that rendered the union of our states forever secure, there could be heard the low mutterings and tremblings of the volcano that four years later was to break forth, casting ruin and infamy upon many a fair name. Dissentions had arisen in the management of the corporations. Those who had been connected with the Credit Mobilier from an early period, becoming discouraged at receiving no returns for their investments, sullenly held back, until it seemed as though the whole scheme must prove a disastrous failure; but when a new life was given the enterprise through the connection and personal influence of a new class of men; when it seemed as though success might crown their efforts; when in fact large returns were insured them, none more eager than these to step forward and assert their claims to the profits which they attempted before to destroy, and which in justice belonged to others.

As we have seen before, the Credit Mobilier passed into the hands of the principal stockholders of the Union Pacific Railroad in the early part of the year 1864, and that it took the active management of the Hoxie contract, so called, in March, 1865. Throughout that summer the Company worked upon that contract, but it soon became apparent to all that even then the work must prove a failure, and that the Credit Mobilier could not carry it on to success, unless new life, new energy, and a great increase of capital could be secured. This certain failure which stared them in the face, and which none could avoid comprehending, was the result of the peculations and jobs that were being carried on by those in charge of the companies. The object of every one, from Mr. Durant down to the common workman, was to grow rich at the expense of the company; and every one was interested in some manner of job by which the company was grossly robbed. Durant was a man of great extravagance, and he cared not for the expenses incurred, so long as he could reap the benefit from every payment. His main idea was to make his profit from the construction; and, to further his own personal advantage, he discouraged none of those schemes by which the company was defrauded, so long as he could share the returns. Under such management, it was no wonder that failure was certain. Not only were new life, energy, and capital necessary, but honesty and integrity as well.

It was thus, while the fate of the Union Pacific Railroad was trembling in the balance, that, in September, 1865, after the most earnest solicitation and appeals to his patriotism, Mr. Oakes Ames, of Massachusetts, a member of Congress, was persuaded to embark in the enterprise. Mr. Ames was a man of very large means, of undoubted integrity, and possessed of the most wonderful energy. His entry into this work was with his whole heart and strength. His first investment, for himself and family, was more than a million dollars. From this time forward he became identified with the building of the road; no labor too arduous, no sacrifice too great, no risk too hazardous; he felt confident of ultimate success, and he lost no opportunity to urge his personal friends to join him in the enterprise. He desired to have associated with him men of means and influence, men whose names would inspire confidence and give to the enterprise a stability of character and standing that would induce others to join with them. He went to his personal friends and, meeting all their objections, induced them to put their money in the road. He went to his friends in Congress and demonstrated to them the great necessity for the road, and some did join with him, and others promised. At this time Congress had no measure before it affecting the Pacific roads; the last legislation had been fourteen months prior to the first connection of Mr. Ames with the Credit Mobilier or the Pacific road. Every act of legislation they desired had already been granted; they had nothing to ask of Congress, and every department of government was so fully in accord and sympathy with the undertaking that there was not the slightest cause to fear any unfriendly legislation. The government was clamorous to have the work completed, and was ready to grant any further concessions that might be requisite to the building of the road. The popular feeling throughout the whole country was so strongly in favor of the early completion of the road that no man would have risked his reputation and standing among his constituents by having attempted to retard the progress of the road. Under these circumstances, Mr. Ames felt no compunction in asking members of Congress to join with him.

Through the years 1865, 1866, and the first part of 1867, the Credit Mobilier continued to work upon the building of the road. The original contract of Hoxie had been extended to the one hundredth meridian, a distance of two hundred and forty-seven miles, and the company still continued to work on the road beyond that point. The Credit Mobilier had as yet paid no dividends. On the contrary, their entire capital, amounting now to $3,750,000, had been swallowed up in the construction of the road. They had been compelled to take the securities of the Union Pacific Railroad Company in payment of work, and no market could be found for them. Efforts had been made to get contractors to build the road, without avail. Mr. Durant had quarrelled with members of the Credit Mobilier, and had been ousted from the direction of the Company, and he determined that the Credit Mobilier should never have another contract for building the road; and, with his influence, as an officer and stockholder in the Union Pacific Railroad Company, and the power of the courts, this he prevented. In August, 1867, a compromise, or at least the nature of one, was concluded, by which Mr. Oakes Ames took his great contract for building 667 miles of the road at a cost of a little more than $47,000,000. Two months later, as we have seen, this contract was assigned to the seven trustees, for certain purposes and uses. About February, 1867, the capital of the Credit Mobilier was increased 50 per cent., or from $2,500,000 to $3,750,000; and it was decided to apportion this to the then stockholders *pro rata* with the stock they then held. This increase of capital was deemed so absolutely necessary that, as an inducement to take it, the company gave as a bonus $1,000 in Union Pacific bonds, for every $1,000 of the additional stock taken. But so low was the confidence, not only of the public, but the stockholders themselves, that many declined taking the new stock, even declaring that they would rather lose their present investment than to sink another dollar in the enterprise. Thus a few shares of the stock remained in the hands of the company undisposed of, there being in all 650 shares. During all the time intervening prior to the execution of the Oakes Ames contract, Mr. Ames had been endeavoring to secure the co-operation of every man of influence with whom he came in contact, seeking to sell them an interest in the Credit Mobilier, and he secured promises from many. After the great contract had been assigned to the trustees and work fairly commenced, and it was seen that large profits would be likely to accrue, then there became a demand for the stock. Mr. Ames, on his return to Congress in the fall of 1867, made arrangements to transfer the stock, as soon as he could obtain it from the company, to such as he had agreed should have it, and also spoke to others regarding it. In the winter of 1867-68, a meeting of the principal stockholders of the Credit Mobilier was held at the Fifth Avenue Hotel in New York, at which time Mr. Ames made the request that the 650 shares of stock then belonging

to the Company be transferred to him, that he
might fulfil the obligations he had made with his
various friends. Mr. T. C. Durant stated he also
had made numerous engagements with his friends,
and demanded that the stock be transferred to him.
Mr. H. S. McComb made a demand to have 250
shares transferred to him, together with the 50 per
cent. increase, making 375 shares in all. His claim
was that he had agreed to take 250 shares of the old
stock on March 3, 1866, and that he now demanded
the stock with all the rights which accrued to it.
This was a claim that none of the other stockholders would recognize, and a great deal of discussion
arose over it. It was finally agreed that the
stock should be divided between Mr. Durant and
Mr. Ames, the former to have 370 shares, and
the latter 280 shares. This arrangement was
agreed to by Mr. McComb, but the president was
unwilling to transfer the stock upon the verbal
assent of Mr. McComb, and so the following
agreement was entered into by these principal stockholders : —

We, the undersigned, stockholders of the Credit
Mobilier of America, understanding that $65,000
of the capital stock of this company, held in trust
by the president, has been promised certain
parties by T. C. Durant and Oakes Ames, do
hereby consent to advise the transfer of said stock
to such parties as they, the said Durant and
Ames, have agreed upon and designate, say to

Durant parties $37,000, and Ames parties $28,000.

JOHN DUFF,	JOHN B. ALLEY,
THOMAS C. DURANT,	C. S. BUSHNELL,
J. BARDWELL,	SIDNEY DILLON,
OAKES AMES,	H. S. MCCOMB,

OLIVER AMES.

The undersigned stockholders of the Credit Mobilier of America recommend the issue to Hon. Oakes Ames, trustee, of ninety-three (93) shares of the capital stock of this company at par.

T. C. DURANT,	S. HOOPER & Co.
C. S. BUSHNELL,	J. BARDWELL,
OAKES AMES,	JOHN DUFF,
OLIVER AMES,	WM. H. MACY,

C. A. LOMBARD.

Mr. McComb says he never read this paper which he signed, but the facts have been clearly shown that he at first refused to sign it, and stated his reasons, claiming that the paper failed to recognize any claim which he had made; but at last he did sign it, fully understanding all that it contained.

This division of those shares shows the manner in which Mr. Ames secured the shares which he had sold to his friends, and in taking them from the Company paid their par value to the Company. They were then no longer the property of the Company, but the property of Mr. Ames, and the Company had no further control.

This division did not tend to lesson the hostility between Mr. McComb and the Credit Mobilier. He still insisted that the 375 shares of stock belonged to him, and maintained his demand for that, together with all the dividends that had been declared upon it, and before the year was closed he commenced a suit against the Company and its officers for the recovery of the stock, to his individual use. In support of this claim affidavits were filed, during the summer of 1872, alleging that the stock had been set apart by the Credit Mobilier to Mr. Ames for the express purpose of distributing to members of Congress, with the object of creating in them such an interest in the road that they could be depended upon in all cases where legislation should come before Congress ; that Mr. Ames had received the stock for that purpose, and had used it for the purpose of corrupting members of Congress ; that while he had sold it to those members, he had sold it at a price far below its actual value, thereby making it in reality a gift to them to that extent, and in his affidavits he mentioned a long list of congressmen who had been selected, and to whom the stock had been transferred. This list, which he claimed had been furnished him by Mr. Ames, contained the names of some who had never been mentioned in connection with the Credit Mobilier, and who never became interested in it in any way ; and, as additional evidence upon this claim of bribery, Mr. McComb filed letters, purporting to have been written by Mr. Ames, and in which he-said he had given the stock to such and such congressmen, that he had given it where it would do the most good, and other expressions of like import. It may be important, in what is to follow, to understand the relations of this suit which Mr. McComb brought. In the early part of 1866, Mr. H. G. Fant, a banker in Washington, and a friend of Mr. McComb, concluded to invest $25,000 in Credit Mobilier stock, and asked Mr. McComb to subscribe that amount for him, and draw on him for the money with which to pay for the shares. On the 3d of March, 1866, Mr. McComb made the subscription for 250 shares at par, and gave to the treasurer of the Credit Mobilier a draft on Mr. Fant for $25,000. A few days later, Mr. McComb was informed that the draft had been protested, whereupon he wrote to Mr. Fant asking an explanation. Mr. Fant replied that owing to certain losses which he had suffered in his business, he could not spare the money. He came to New York in a few days, and requested that his offer be left open for a short time, and perhaps he would take the stock. The Credit Mobilier at that time was in great need of funds, and such an acquisition would be of the greatest benefit to them, and so they gladly extended the time. Thirty days passed, but still nothing was done. Some time after this, Mr. McComb desired that the draft be returned to him, and that the whole transaction be cancelled, and that the stock be returned to the treasury. This was done; the sale was rendered void, and Mr. McComb's draft was returned to him. Nothing

more was heard of this claim for more than a year
and a half after this. When the contract had been
let to Mr. Ames, and his agreement given that the
stockholders of the Credit Mobilier were to share
those profits, the stock of the Credit Mobilier
became valuable. One day Mr. McComb entered
the office and spoke to Mr. Alley, Mr. Durant, and
another of the directors, and said he wanted a talk
with them upon a certain subject, and asked when
they could hear him. The following day was
appointed, and at that meeting Mr. McComb made
his claim that the old subscription he had made in
March, 1866, was still open, and he proposed to pay
for the stock now, and asked that it be assigned to
him. The proposal was so preposterous that the
others laughed at him, even his friend Durant.
They told him that that had long ago been cancelled, and that his draft had been given up to him,
and that at his own request all obligations against
him by the Company, by reason of that subscription,
had been annulled. McComb claimed, however,
that the draft had not been returned, and that he
had the right to the stock. Of course, every director refused to recognize so baseless a claim. He
threatened suit to recover it; but no heed was taken
of it. At the meeting in New York, in the early
part of 1868, when the stock in the treasury
was divided between Mr. Durant and Mr. Ames,
Mr. McComb was present, and again asserted his
claim to the stock, and saying that he, as well as the
others, had promised the stock to his friends; but

finally, as we have seen, he consented to the division of the stock between Mr. Durant and Mr. Ames, thus effectually relinquishing every right to the stock which he had claimed. But, even after this, he insisted on having the stock, and still threatened suit unless it was given him. No attention was paid to him.

During the same year he did commence a suit, alleging the value of the stock to be very great, and that he was entitled to the dividends declared. The dividends which he alleged had been paid were very largely in excess of all that were declared upon all the contracts for the building of the Pacific road. This suit dragged along through the courts until the year 1872, when more desperate measures were resorted to to secure a settlement. Mr. McComb, through his counsel, Judge Black, came to Mr. Alley, and said that the best thing that could be done was to settle the suits, as Mr. McComb had letters from Mr. Ames, which established the proof of bribery on the part of Mr. Ames, and that if those letters were made public it would ruin many a man then high in official position, and bring untold disgrace upon the country. Mr. Alley replied that it was impossible that Mr. Ames could ever have written any such letters—he had too much faith in Mr. Ames to even consider such a thought—and refused absolutely to entertain the proposition of a settlement. Mr. Black came again, and said that he would settle all matters for $100,000; that he knew the contents of those letters, and that there was the most convincing evidence in them not only against Mr. Ames, but against many prominent men, and among them one of his dearest friends. So earnest was he, and so positive, that Mr. Alley laid the matter before Mr. Ames. Mr. Ames asserted positively that he never had entertained any thought of bribery; that he was an honorable man, and that never had he attempted in the least to influence the acts of any man in Congress by gifts, or by anything of pecuniary value; whatever he had done he was perfectly willing the whole world should know; that he never had written any letters such as Mr. McComb claimed to hold, nor was he aware of any expression in any letter he had ever written which could be tortured into such an idea, for certainly not the faintest thought of any such conduct had ever entered his mind. He told Mr. Alley to say to Judge Black that he defied him in any such attempt to blackmail him or those he was associated with. A third time Judge Black came around, attempted to effect a settlement on the basis of surrendering the letters, and ending the suit. So great was the confidence of those associated with Mr. Ames in his honor that all attempts to arrange a settlement failed. At last the letters were produced in court, and before long found their way to the public through the New York *Sun*.

We present copies of these letters as they appeared before the public, and then shall take occasion to comment upon them.

It should be remembered that these letters were all written by Mr. Ames in reply to letters written him by Mr. McComb, and that all the matters referred to had been spoken of by Mr. McComb. At the time that Mr. McComb had assented to the division of the stock of the Credit Mobilier between Mr. Durant and Mr. Ames, he made the claim that he had promised a part of his stock to certain of his friends, and when he could not obtain the stock, he wished Mr. Ames to deliver a portion of the stock assigned to him, to Mr. Bayard and Mr. Fowler; and now he had written to Mr. Ames to know why the stock had not been delivered. There was also much complaint made both by Mr. McComb and Mr. Durant, and by their friends, that Mr. Ames was selling this stock very largely among his own personal friends from Massachusetts, thus seeking to keep the control of the corporations in his own hands. This circumstance had, previous to this, led to many angry assertions, but Mr. Ames had always declared that such was not his intention. It was the desire of all parties that the stock should be distributed over as large a part of the country as could be, in order that all sections should have an interest in pushing forward this great national work. It was a work in which the whole country was deeply interested. In Mr. McComb's letter to Mr. Ames, January 23, 1868, he insisted that Mr. Ames should distribute the stock not wholly to his own New England friends, but to serve all alike. All of this stock had long before been sold by Mr. Ames to these parties, and it was for the purpose of fulfilling his obligations to them that the stock had been secured by Mr. Ames. These sales had been agreed upon during the early part of 1867, some months before the Ames contract had been executed; but the parties who had contracted for the stock were not anxious to take it while it was not worth par—the price which they had agreed to pay. As soon, however, as the Ames contract had gone into effect, and work under it commenced, and it was decided that a dividend be declared, the stock at once rose in value, and by the end of December, 1867, was considerably above par. Then it was that Mr. Ames was literally besieged by members of Congress, who declared that they had agreed to take the stock, and wanted it delivered. Many, indeed, came to him in this way, and asserted positively that he had sold them the stock, when, in point of fact, the only conversation ever held was that when Mr. Ames asked them if they would take some of the stock they replied that "they would see." When they came forward now, and insisted on having the stock, it placed Mr. Ames in a difficult position, and he was forced to decide with whom his engagements had been positive, and with whom they had been only spoken of. It was in this spirit that the first of these letters was written, intending thereby to so present the case to Mr. McComb that he should no longer have occasion to accuse him of favoring any particular section, or his own personal friends.

We present the letter in full:

WASHINGTON, Jan. 25, 1868.

H. S. McComb, Esq.,

DEAR SIR:—Yours of the 23d is at hand, in which you say Senators Bayard and Fowler have written you in relation to their stock. I have spoken to Fowler, but not to Bayard; I have never been introduced to Bayard, but will see him soon. You say I must not put too much in one locality. I have assigned as far as I have gone to, 4 from Mass., 1 from N. H., 1 Delaware, 1 Tenn., 1 Ohio, 2 Penn., 1 Ind., 1 Maine, and I have three to place, which I shall place where they will do most good to us. I am here on the spot, and can better judge where they should go. I think after this dividend is paid we should make our capital 4.000.000, and distribute the new stock where it will protect us—let them have the stock at par, and profits made in the future; the 50 per cent. increase on the old stock, I want for distribution here, and soon. Alley is opposed to the division of the bonds; says we will need them, &c., &c. I should think we ought to be able to spare them, with Alley and Cisco on the finance committee; we used to be able to borrow when we had no credit and debts pressing. We are now out of debt and in good credit—what say you about the bond dividend? —a part of the purchasers here are poor, and want their bonds to sell to enable them to meet their payment on the stock in the C. M. I have told them what they would get as dividend, and they expect, I think, the bonds the parties receive as the 80 per cent. dividend; we better give them the bonds—it will not amount to anything with us. Some of the large holders will not care whether they have the bonds or certificates, or they will lend their bonds to the company as they have done before, or lend them money. Quigley has been here, and we have got that $\frac{1}{10}$ that was Underwood's. I have taken half, Quigley $\frac{1}{4}$, and you $\frac{1}{4}$. J. Carter wants a part of it; at some future day we will surrender a part to him.

Yours truly,

OAKES AMES.

In interpreting any letter we should always ascertain the style and character of the writer. What one man would do another would not. One man may be open and free in his utterances, while another is guarded and careful in all he says. Those who have known Mr. Ames will bear out the assertion that he never stopped to consider the result of what he said or did. He was not a finely educated man — he was not capable of drawing fine distinctions in the meaning of words. To those who knew him, these letters will show the man — open, plain and blunt — as he always was. When, therefore, he was accused by Mr. McComb of giving the stock only to certain personal friends, he naturally replied that he had "assigned" it to such and such persons, covering the entire country; he had made his decision as to whom the stock belonged, by reason of prior engagements. And he had done this among men of influence, men whose names would add dignity, stability and strength to the enterprise; whose names connected with it would add confidence among their constituents, and thus in reality "do most good" to the early completion of the road.

He wanted the balance of the increase of stock for "distribution." He had sold it and the parties who had bought it wanted it, as appears very strongly from the latter part of his letter, where he says the "purchasers" want the dividends to meet their payments on the stock. There was much opposition to declaring these dividends, and, as Mr. Ames says, this came from Mr. Alley, who insisted that before the work was done they might need all their funds — and in this he was right.

Mr. McComb was well aware of the condition in which Mr. Ames was situated; he knew that the stock had been long before sold these parties, at a time when the stock was in reality below par, and here certainly no inference was made that he was selling it below par. The last clauses of this letter have no reference to the Credit Mobilier, but to a railroad in the West in which they were both interested.

The next letter is as follows:

WASHINGTON, Jan. 30, 1868.

H. S. McComb,

DEAR SIR:—Yours of the 28th is at hand, enclosing a letter from, or rather to, Mr. King. I don't fear any investigation here. What some of Durant's friends may do in N. Y. courts can't be counted upon with any certainty. You do not understand, by your letter, what I have done, & am to do with my sales of stock. You say none to N. Y. I have placed some with New York, or have agreed to. You must remember it was nearly all placed as you saw on the list in N. Y., &

there was but 6 or 8 m. for me to place. I could not give all the world all they might want out of that. You would not want me to offer less than 1 m. to any one. We allow Durant to place 58,000 to some 3 or 4 of his friends, or keep it himself.

I have used this where it will produce most good to us, I think. In view of King's letter and Washburne's move here, I go in for making our bond dividend in full. We can do it with perfect safety. I understand the opposition to it comes from Alley; he is on the finance com'ee and can raise money easy if we come short, which I don't believe we shall; & if we do we can loan our bonds to the company, or loan them the money we get from the bonds. The contract calls for the division, and I say have it. When shall I see you in Washington?

Yours truly,

OAKES AMES.

We stand about like this:

Bonds 1st mortgage, rec'd on 525 miles at 16 m.	8,400,000
" " " " " 15 " " 48 m.	720,000
" " " " " 100 " " 48 m.	4,800,000
	13,920,000
10,000,000 sold & to sell, to pay our debts,	10,000,000
	3,920,000
80 p'r cent. dividend on 3,700,000 C. M. of A.	3,000,000
	920,000
Gov't bond received this day, - - - - -	960,000
Due for transportation, 400 m., one-half cash,	200,000
	2,080,000

In addition to this we can draw Gov't bond for ⅔ of the work in advance of track, if we desire it.

Oakes Ames' list of names as showed to-day to me for C. M.:
 Blaine, of Maine, 3,000.
 Patterson, N. Hamp. 3,000.
 Wilson, Mass., 2.
 Painter Rep. for Inq., 3.
 S. Colfax, Speaker, 2.
 Elliott, Mass., 3.
 Dawes,   "   2.
 Boutwell, " 2.
 Bingham & Garfield, Ohio.
 Scofield & Kelley, Penn.
 Fowler, Tenn.
  Feb. 1, 1868.

This list of names attached to this letter is in the handwriting of Mr. McComb himself, and he says he wrote them as Mr. Ames read them to him from his memorandum-book. It was not pretended, even by Mr. McComb, in his evidence before the committee, that this list was written by Mr. Ames, though in his affidavits in the suit it was set out to that effect; and it was this list, as well as the letters, which produced the great commotion through the country. In no other place in their correspondence were any names mentioned. But this list is extremely faulty, containing names of men who never contracted for a share of stock, even in the most indirect manner.

The above letter is written in reply to another complaining letter from Mr. McComb, in which he referred to an investigation, to which Mr. Ames merely replies that he does not fear any investigation.

He was sure that an investigation could do no harm, for all transactions had been honorable, and he was willing they should be known.

In fact, when a motion was made in the House for an investigation, no particular opposition was made to it, and especially by those who have been named as takers of these bribes. The records of Congress show that of all these men who have been named as holding the stock, Mr. Brooks is the only one who was opposed to it, or who did not vote for it, and he did not, for special reasons which he assigned, but was not opposed to an investigation. The remarks which were made to the former letter will apply here, as to the distribution of the stock. The Washburne move spoken of was the motion for the investigation, which we have seen was voted for by all these men who were interested in Credit Mobilier. If, then, this stock was distributed for the purpose of influencing the legislative action of these men, how utterly it failed! He "used the stock where it would produce most good," but that was among those men who, as said in reference to the former letter, would add dignity, stability and strength to the organization. No reference was intended to legislative action, for none was contemplated, none was feared, and had any been made it would not have received opposition. In this letter he again refers to the bond dividend, again speaks of Mr. Alley's opposition to it, but thinks it can be made with safety, for should they need money, it could easily be raised with such a man as Mr. Alley on the finance committee, and then says that his contract called for the dividend, and he wanted it. He then makes a brief statement, showing how they would stand after making the dividend.

WASHINGTON, Feb. 22, 1868.

H. S. McComb, Esq.,

DEAR SIR:—Yours of the 21st is at hand; am glad to hear that you are getting along so well with Mr. West, and hope you will bring it out all satisfactory, so that it will be so rich that we can not help going into it. I return you the paper by mail that you ask for. You ask me if I will sell some of my U. P. R. R. stock. I will sell some of it at par, C. M. of A. I don't care to sell. I hear that Mr. Bates offered his at $300, but I don't want Bates to sell out. I think Grimes may sell a part of his at $350. I want that $14,000 increase of the Credit Mobilier to sell here. We want more friends in this Congress, & if a man will look into the law (& it is difficult for them to do it unless they have an interest to do so), he can not help being convinced that we should not be interfered with. Hope to see you here or at N. Y. the 11th.

Yours truly,
OAKES AMES.

The first part of this letter relates to matters entirely foreign to the Credit Mobilier. In Mr. McComb's letter, the question was asked if Mr. Ames would sell his U. P. R. R. stock. This he did not care to do, and then he speaks of the price of Credit Mobilier stock, in reply to Mr. McComb's questions; as to these values we shall speak further on, only here let us say that while the price of the stock at the date of this letter may have been as specified, it is by no means a conclusion that that was its price before December, when the stock was sold these members of Congress. The only words that reflect upon Mr. Ames are in relation to "friends in Congress," but as we have already spoken of this, and shall have occasion to refer to it again, we need here only refer to our former remarks, asserting that it would be only a natural consequence, for a man of his bluntness, to make use of such expressions. Then, too, it should be borne in mind that these letters were written by Mr. Ames for the very purpose of quieting the complaints of Mr. McComb, and of showing to him that the writer was not working for his own personal gratification, but for the best good of all those with whom he was associated.

The effect of these letters upon the public mind was like wildfire. A presidential campaign was in progress, and most of the men whose names were given were candidates for office. Without stopping to consider, they denied all and every connection with the Credit Mobilier, — denied that they had ever invested a dollar in the enterprise, or ever received a dollar from such investment, either directly or indirectly.

These denials are all matters of history, and do not properly belong to a work of this nature. The papers of those days were filled with the allegations of corruption and bribery. The names of those who had stood highest in the national councils were bandied about and made by-words for infamy. Those who denied their connection did so boldly, firmly believing that, when investigation came, as they knew it must come, Mr. Ames would help them through, and clear them from all blame. As long as it was through their connection with Mr. Ames that they had become involved in these investments, they calculated that he would stand by them, and assume the responsibility, and by his testimony corroborate their denials. But they learned that Oakes Ames would tell the truth, and as a consequence their denials were found to be false. The denials served however a temporary purpose, and all was moving along smoothly, until Congress met in December, 1872, when the whole country seemed to unite in the demand for an investigation of these charges. There was a frenzy of excitement over it. The disgrace which had come upon the country was so great that it was imperative something should be done to disprove these allegations of corruption in our national councils, or else to punish the guilty as they deserved.

As soon as the session of Congress which convened in December, 1872, was opened, the Speaker, James G. Blaine, called Mr. S. S. Cox to the chair, and, from his position on the floor, spoke of these rumors that had appeared in the press throughout the country, and asked that a committee be appointed to investigate the matters therein alleged. No objection was made to the motion, which, as passed, was as follows:

Whereas accusations have been made in the public press, founded on the alleged letters of Oakes Ames, a Representative from Massachusetts, and upon the alleged affidavit of Henry S. McComb, a citizen of Wilmington, in the State of Delaware, to the effect that members of this House were bribed by Oakes Ames to perform certain legislative acts for the benefit of the Union Pacific Railway Company, by presents of stock in the Credit Mobilier of America, or by presents of a valuable character derived therefrom : Therefore

Resolved, That a special committee of five members be appointed by the Speaker *pro tempore*, whose duty it shall be to investigate and ascertain whether any member of this House was bribed by Oakes Ames, or any other person or corporation, in any matter touching his legislative duty.

Resolved further, That the committee have the right to employ a stenographer, and that they be empowered to send for persons and papers.

The following committee was appointed :

LUKE P. POLLAND, of Vermont,
NATHANIEL P. BANKS, of Massachusetts,
JAMES B. BECK, of Kentucky,
WILLIAM E. NIBLACK, of Indiana,
GEORGE W. McCRARY, of Iowa.

This committee entered upon their duties as soon as all the preliminaries could be arranged, and conducted their examination each day until about the middle of the February following, having, in the meantime, examined every person who had any knowledge of the subject of their inquiries. Every member of Congress whose name had been mentioned as having had an interest in the Credit Mobilier came before the committee and gave his testimony. In only a few instances did any of these witnesses deny having any connection with the Credit Mobilier, or that they had engaged to take stock from Mr. Ames. For some time after the committee commenced their investigation they met with closed doors, as is the usual practice of such committees; but owing to the garbled reports that appeared in the press, and the great interest which spread through the country, the doors of the committee-room were thrown open, and from this time the investigation became public, and full reports of the proceedings appeared in the daily papers throughout the land Whatever may be said of the work of this committee, no one can charge that they attempted anything, in their examinations of the witnesses, but to arrive at the exact truth. The examination was thorough and exhaustive, and on the 18th of February, 1873, they submitted their report to the House. Much of the substance of the report will appear in the following pages, in so far as it relates to the connection with the members of Congress.

During the progress of this investigation, at the time it was proposed to make the investigation open and public, Mr. Wilson of Indiana, on January 6, 1873, presented the following resolution, which was adopted:

Resolved, That a select committee of five members of this House be appointed by the Speaker, and such committee be, and is hereby instructed to enquire whether or not any person connected with the organization or association commonly known as the "Credit Mobilier," now holds any of the bonds of the Union Pacific Railroad Company, for the payment of which, or the interest thereon, the United States is in any way liable; and whether or not, such holders, if any, or their assignees, of such bonds, are holders in good faith, and for value, or procured the same illegally or by fraud, and whether or not the United States may properly refuse to pay interest thereon, or the principal thereof, when the same shall become due, and whether or not any relinquishment of first mortgage lien that may heretofore have been made by the United States with reference to the bonds of said Railroad Company may be set aside, and to inquire into the character and purpose of such organization, and what officers of the United States or members of Congress have at any time been connected therewith, what connection it had with the contracts for the construction of said Union Pacific Railroad Company, and to report the facts to this House, together with such bill as may be necessary to protect the interests of the United States on account of any of the bonds of the class hereinbefore referred to; and said committee is authorized to send for persons and papers, and to report any time.

On the following day the Speaker appointed as that committee

J. M. WILSON, of Indiana,
SAMUEL SHELLABARGER, of Ohio,
GEORGE F. HOAR, of Massachusetts,
THOMAS SWANN, of Maryland,
H. W. SLOCUM, of New York.

On the 10th January the committee met and commenced the investigation, and continued that investigation until the 19th of February, and submitted their report to the House on the 20th of February.

From this time on there were two committees of investigation at work upon the Credit Mobilier, and its connection with the building of the Union Pacific Railroad. Their objects were different, but were intended to cover the entire ground. By an examination of the resolutions creating them, it will be seen that the first committee appointed, and generally known as the "Polland Committee," from its chairman, had to investigate the connection of the various members of Congress with the Credit Mobilier, and discover, if possible, whether any bribery had been used by "Mr. Ames, or any other person or corporation," in order to procure the influence of members of Congress in legislation to be brought before Congress; while the other committee, known as the "Wilson Committee," from its chairman, was to investigate the connection of the Credit Mobilier with the construction of the Union Pacific Railroad, and to discover if any illegal means had been used whereby the government had been defrauded, and to ascertain whether the government could recede from the agreement to accept a second lien for the loan of its bonds to the road.

We have, in the former part of this work, had occasion to deal almost entirely with the province of this latter, the "Wilson Committee," and it will be unnecessary now to go over any of the details of that investigation. The work of that committee was intended to be thorough, as was that of the Polland committee. Yet, when we come to the *report* as written by the committee, we must dissent from the conclusions reached by them. They could not, at least they did not, understand the relations existing between the Credit Mobilier and the seven trustees, and the Union Pacific road. In this they were entirely at fault, and it was not surprising that they should be, for to this day, those who have even given the subject much close attention, have failed to understand the nice distinctions that existed. The Credit Mobilier had nothing to do with the Ames contract; it never received a dividend from that contract, and no dividend was ever declared by the Credit Mobilier, excepting one of 12 per cent. from the money paid it by the trustees. The committee did not discern that the Credit Mobilier had lost its entire capital in the construction of the road; or that it had been cheated and robbed by those who first had its management; they failed absolutely to understand the relations of the government to the Pacific roads, and imagined that the government had loaned them a large amount of money for the construction of the road, when in fact the government had never loaned them one cent. The utmost that had been done was to loan them the credit of the government, it being in reality the same as an accommodation note, which if paid when due would be no loss to any one, and to secure this payment the government had a second mortgage on the road. They could not comprehend the mighty difficulties that encompassed the road on every side during its construction, but they judged it as though all those great obstacles had been removed, and the road was being constructed at the time the report was being made. They declared that so great had been the fraud practiced on the government by these proceedings, that the goverment would have a right, but for the presence of a few innocent stockholders, to declare the franchises forfeited. The committee could not understand the relations of cost and profits, and in their attempt to show some great fraud, made out the profits of construction to amount to more than $43,000,000, with a cash value of some $23,000,000, when the cash value of the profit actually made was but a trifle over $8,000,000. The minds of the committee were so evidently biased that they could see nothing in its true light, could understand nothing as it actually was, but thought (probably because so many of their constituents did, and they were very anxious to be returned to Congress) that there was fraud on every hand, and that no men could carry through so gigantic a scheme and remain honest. The committee concluded their report by recommending the passage of a bill, which we understand was the product of the able mind of Hon. George F. Hoar, of Massachusetts, which instructed the attorney-general to institute a suit against every one who had ever received any of the dividends declared from the construction of the road, to recover such dividends. The bill is a model for future generations to follow, and will ever stand as a most beautiful combination of English words, but it would require two or three acts of Congress to understand its objects and intent.

In consequence of this report, Congress, in 1876, instructed the attorney-general to institute a suit in equity for the recovery of all property wrongfully appropriated.

The statute under which the suit was brought authorized a moneyed decree in favor of the Railroad Company for money due for capital stock, or money or property received from it on fraudulent contracts, or for money or property which ought in equity to belong to the company; and it authorized a decree in favor of the United States or the company for money, bonds, or lands wrongfully received from the United States which ought in equity to be paid or accounted for.

The Supreme Court of the United States in 1879, has affirmed a decision previously rendered in the United States Circuit Court of Connecticut, upon the suit thus instituted, and has decided that

This bill exhibits no right to relief on the part of the United States founded on the charter contract. The company has constructed its road to completion, keeps it in running order and carries for the government all that is required of it. It owes the government nothing that is due, and the government has the security which by law it provided. Nor does the bill show anything which authorizes the United States, as the depository of a trust, public or private, to sustain the suit.

The Court adds:

The truth is, that the persons who were actually defrauded by these transactions, if any such there be, were the few *bona-fide* holders of the stock of the corporation, who took no part in these proceedings, and had no interest in the fraudulent contracts. But it is not alleged that there were any such.

We need not pursue the report of the Wilson committee any further. We have attempted to show the true relations of the Credit Mobilier and the Union Pacific Railroad, also the relations between the Credit Mobilier and the trustees. We hope we have made the subject plain. The complications were great, the distinctions finely drawn. But the positions taken by the parties at the time have been sustained by the highest court of justice in the world; their position has been declared impregnable, and no court has been found to declare that fraud was used against the government in the construction of the Union Pacific Road.

This was the report of the "Wilson Committee." The evidence has been alluded to, in the former part of this work. Here we leave this portion of the subject, and proceed to the work of the other committee of investigation.

VIII.

THE POLLAND COMMITTEE.

THE first witness examined by the Polland committee (after the statement of James G. Blaine) was Mr. H. S. McComb. His testimony was to the effect that, in conversations with Mr. Ames, admissions were made by Mr. Ames that he had used the stock of the Credit Mobilier for the purpose of influencing members of Congress to vote in the interests of the Union Pacific Railroad; that Mr. Ames had told him that such was his intention in getting the stock, and that once Mr. Ames asked him if he did not consider it a good use of the stock which he gave to Mr. Colfax, then Speaker of the House, in view of the decision or ruling made by him on the Washburne motion. Mr. McComb alleged that, by some parliamentary ruling, the Speaker had killed such motion. The evidence was also positive that Mr. McComb overheard a conversation between Mr. Brooks and Mr. Alley, in which Mr. Brooks demanded the giving to him of fifty shares of the Credit Mobilier stock, and promising, if that was done, that he would look out for the Democratic side of the House, in all legislation concerning the Union Pacific Railroad; and that, in consideration of such promise, Mr. Alley did cause to be issued to Mr. Brooks the fifty shares of stock which he demanded. Mr. McComb's testimony in regard to this was most positive and direct, and he fixed the time within fifty-seven days of when it occurred; that there were several conversations concerning it, but all occurred within this time, which he could fix by the absence of Dr. Durant in Europe, and that he always thought Mr. Alley was taking advantage of such absence, in giving away this stock.

Mr. McComb also produced the letters which we have set out, and commented upon them in an unfavorable light; he claimed that the letters were written in a manner denoting great confidence, such as Mr. Ames had always placed in him; that Mr. Ames had told him many times that he had used the stock assigned him, for the purpose of influencing members of Congress, and that that was the purpose for which the Credit Mobilier had given him the stock; that though he had offered it for par, it was at the time offered worth far more than that.

No other evidence was tendered or produced upon this point, and the entire testimony regarding any admission by Mr. Ames, or any conversations by him, was that of Mr. McComb. His testimony in this respect stands unsupported and alone, except for what color may be given it by the letters which he produced, and which Mr. Ames never denied having written. A large amount of the testimony related to the work of the Credit Mobilier, which we have already considered, and the manner in which members of Congress had invested in the stock; but with the testimony of Mr. McComb, his assertions stand exactly as he left them, to be met and overturned by a multitude of witnesses.

Mr. Ames denies, positively, that he ever had any such conversations with Mr. McComb; denies that he ever made any such admissions; denies that he ever entertained a thought of influencing a member of Congress, in his legislative action; claims that he sold the stock to the several members of Congress at a time when that stock was not above par, at a time when it was being freely offered to the public, without finding a buyer, and that it was sold to those who bought it only upon the representations of Mr. Ames that it would be a good paying investment; that he had no thought of corrupting members, for he had no legislation to ask for, and had no reason to expect any adverse to the interests of the Union Pacific road; that the letters which he had written Mr. McComb were in response to others written by Mr. McComb, and in reply to questions proposed by him; and in view of the struggle Mr. McComb was making to gain possession of this stock, he naturally addressed him in such language as would tell him that he was working for the prosperity and success of an enterprise in which Mr. McComb had a deep interest, like himself. The letters were framed for a specific purpose, and to accomplish a particular end; their bearings were not reflected upon or considered; they were written hastily in the press of business, and in that freedom that usually exists between parties embarked in the same enterprise; that he was never confidential with Mr. McComb, in fact, was opposed to him, in his management of affairs. He made no denial of selling stock to members of Congress, but maintained it was all sold before there had been any increase in the value of that stock, and that he sold it at its full value. Thus the evidence of these two parties stood directly opposed to each other, and it was to be decided which was true.

The evidence of all witnesses was to the effect that the stock was sold by Mr. Ames immediately after the assembling of Congress, in the winter of 1867-68, or even before that,—certainly not later than a few weeks after the opening of Congress. This point we shall refer to further on. The records of Congress showed that no legislation affecting the Pacific roads was before Congress at the time, and that none of importance was brought up for nearly two years after the road was completed. It was shown by five witnesses that the conversations between Mr. Brooks and Mr. Alley could not have occurred; for at the time which was so positively sworn to, Mr. Alley was out west on the line of the road then being built; that Mr. Alley had nothing to do regarding the issue of the stock to Mr. Brooks, as that was a matter decided upon by a large number of the principal stockholders, and all of whom signed an agreement consenting to its sale to Mr. Brooks,—an agreement which Mr. Alley did not sign, but which Mr. McComb did; and that agreement was before the committee; and it was shown that the Speaker, Mr. Colfax, had never made any such ruling as testified to by Mr. McComb, and consequently Mr. Ames could never have made the assertion attributed to him regarding it.

It would, of course, be impossible to set out here all this mass of testimony, nor would it be in accordance with the design of this work. We must content ourselves with a brief review of the testimony concerning each member of Congress whose name was mentioned as a holder of Credit Mobilier stock.

We shall attempt merely to give the result regarding each, excepting in those cases where there were such strong denials of any connection with the stock, and which denials were proved to be false, and also where the committee refer to the evidence in support of their conclusions.

We shall commence with some of the members of the Senate, and first with

JOHN A. LOGAN, OF ILLINOIS.

In December, 1867, Mr. Logan made an arrangement with Mr. Ames to purchase ten shares of Credit Mobilier stock upon Mr. Ames' recommendation that it was valuable. No payment was made in consideration of the agreement, at any time, and no stock was ever delivered. In June, 1868, Mr. Ames stated to Mr. Logan that he had two dividends on his stock in the Credit Mobilier, one of 80 and the other of 60 per cent.; and that, deducting the $1,000 due on the stock, there was a balance in his favor of $329, which was paid Mr. Logan by check on the sergeant-at-arms, which check was paid. On the 10th of July following, Mr. Logan becoming convinced that there might be trouble about it, returned the money to Mr. Ames, stating he had concluded not to take the stock, and there the transaction ended, Mr. Logan having no further interest in it. Mr. Logan at that time was a member of the House.

ROSCOE CONKLING, OF NEW YORK.

Mr. Conkling does not appear to have been connected in any way with the stock of the Credit Mobilier or of the Union Pacific Railroad Company, and consequently could be in no way affected thereby.

HENRY WILSON.

On or about December, 1867, Senator Wilson contracted for 20 shares of the Credit Mobilier stock in behalf of his wife, paying in cash therefor $2,000, receiving a guarantee from Mr. Ames. Mr. Wilson soon became dissatisfied with the transaction, and upon the agreement of Mr. Ames, the sale was thrown up. Mr. Ames returned the $2,000, and Mr. Wilson returned all dividends he had received, and also paid to his wife $814, which she would have been entitled to as dividends. The purchase money belonged to Mrs. Wilson.

JAMES G. BLAINE.

Mr. Ames requested Mr. Blaine to take ten shares of the stock, recommending it as a good investment. Upon consideration Mr. Blaine concluded not to take the stock, and never did take it; never paid or received anything on account of it; and never had any interest, direct or indirect, in Credit Mobilier stock, or stock of the Union Pacific Railroad Company.

HENRY L. DAWES.

In December, 1867, Mr. Dawes made application to Mr. Ames for the purchase of a thousand dollar bond of the Cedar Rapids road of Iowa; but on the recommendation and guarantee of Mr. Ames he took ten shares of Credit Mobilier stock, paid $800 down, and in a few days the balance. In June, 1868, there was a dividend of 60 per cent. paid. Mr. Ames handed him $400, placing the other $200 to his credit on other accounts between them. Some time after, hearing of the litigation concerning the stock, Mr. Dawes desired to rescind the sale, which was done. Mr. Dawes was allowed 10 per cent. for his money, and returned the dividends he had received. He had no other benefit under the contract than to get 10 per cent. for his money, and after the settlement had no further interest in the stock.

GLENNI W. SCOFIELD, OF PENNSYLVANIA.

In December, 1867, Mr. Scofield applied to Mr. Ames to purchase some Cedar Rapids stock, when Mr. Ames suggested that he buy some Credit Mobilier stock, and explaining that it was a contracting company organized under the laws of Pennsylvania, and was engaged in building the Union Pacific Railroad, and said he would like to see some Pennsylvanians in it, and guaranteed Mr. Scofield eight per cent. on his investment. Mr. Scofield, a little later, paid $1,041 for ten shares, and received upon the same the dividend of eighty per cent. in bonds, and also the cash dividend of sixty per cent. Before the close of the session Mr. Scofield, for some reason, became disinclined to hold the stock, and made arrangements with Mr. Ames to rescind the sale, which was done, and thereafter Mr. Scofield had no further interest.

JOHN A. BINGHAM, OF OHIO.

In December, 1867, Mr. Ames advised Mr. Bingham to invest in Credit Mobilier stock, assuring him it would pay him good dividends. About February 1st, 1868, Mr. Bingham purchased twenty shares, paying the par value thereof in cash. Mr. Ames received all the dividends, and turned the most over to Mr. Bingham, retaining some. A final settlement was made in 1872, and in that Mr. Bingham received all dividends due him, Mr. Ames retaining the twenty shares of Credit Mobilier, and accounting therefor. Mr. Bingham was accounted the owner of the stock, and received all the dividends that were declared upon it.

WILLIAM D. KELLEY, OF PENNSYLVANIA.

In the early part of December, 1867, Mr. Ames agreed to sell Mr. Kelley ten shares of Credit Mobilier stock at par and interest from July 1, 1867. Mr. Kelley was not then prepared to pay for the stock,

and Mr. Ames agreed to carry it until he could pay
for it. On the 3d of January, 1868, there was a dividend of eighty per cent. on Credit Mobilier stock in
Union Pacific bonds. Mr. Ames received the bonds,
as the stock stood in his name, and sold them for
ninety-seven per cent. of their face. In June, 1868,
there was a cash dividend of sixty per cent., which
Mr. Ames also received. The proceeds of the
bonds sold, and the cash received, by Mr. Ames,
amounted to $1,376. The par value of the stock,
and the interest thereon from the July previous,
amounted to $1,047; so, after paying for the stock,
there was a balance of dividends due Mr. Kelley of
$329. On the 23d day of June, 1868, Mr. Ames
gave Mr. Kelley a check for that sum on the
sergeant-at-arms of the House of Representatives,
and Mr. Kelley received the money thereon. The
committee were of the opinion that Mr. Kelley
understood that the money he thus received was a
balance of dividends due him after paying for the
stock. In September, 1868, Mr. Kelley received
from Mr. Ames $750 in money, which was understood between them as an advance to be paid out of
dividends. There is, however, an entire variance
in the testimony of these two men as to what the
transaction between them was; but the committee
were unanimous in finding the facts as stated above.

GEORGE S. BOUTWELL, OF MASSACHUSETTS

was among those who have been said to be holders
of stock in the Credit Mobilier; but he never had

any stock, or any dividend thereon; no money was paid by him for stock, or received by him for the same.

B. F. BOYER, OF PHILADELPHIA

was a member of the House from 1865 to 1869. In his testimony he says: "I took the stock in my own name, and have so held it ever since, as the books will show. I held seventy-five shares as my own, and twenty-five shares for my wife, making 100 shares in all. I always considered it a legitimate stock operation, and never denied having made the investment. It did not interfere with my duties as a member of Congress." "No one connected with the Credit Mobilier, or the Union Pacific Railroad, ever directly, or indirectly, expressed, or in any way hinted, that my services as a member of Congress were expected in behalf of either corporation in consideration of the stock I obtained, and certainly no such services were ever rendered." "It was, in my judgment, both honest and honorable, and consistent with my position as a member of Congress; and, as the investment turned out to be profitable, my only regret is that it was no larger in amount."

JAMES A. BAYARD, OF DELAWARE

was among those mentioned to whom stock was to be sold. In his letter to Mr. McComb he refers the whole matter to his son; but finding out afterwards that it might be an arrangement affecting his action as a senator he positively declined having anything to do with it.

JAMES BROOKS, OF NEW YORK.

This case differs much from any other already given. Mr. Brooks was always a warm advocate of the Pacific roads, both in Congress and in the public press. After the Credit Mobilier was obtained for the construction of the Pacific railroad, Mr. Brooks made efforts in connection with Dr. Durant to obtain subscriptions to its stock, and also spoke with Dr. Durant about taking $15,000 or $20,000 of the stock himself; but no arrangement was made by which either party would be bound. In December, 1867, after the value of the stock had greatly increased, Mr. Brooks demanded of the Credit Mobilier Company the transfer of 200 shares, which he claimed he had made arrangements for. Some difficulty arose, but the matter was finally compromised by Mr. Brooks receiving 100 shares of the Credit Mobilier stock, $5,000 of Union Pacific bonds, and $20,000 of Union Pacific stock. Mr. Brooks was, however, a government director of the road, and, as the law provided that such directors should not be stockholders in the road, he could not hold this stock, but had it transferred to his son-in-law, Charles H. Neilson. The whole negotiation was conducted by Mr. Brooks, and Neilson had nothing to do with it except to receive the transfer. The $10,000 to pay for the hundred shares was paid by Mr. Brooks, and he received the $5,000 which came with the stock. The dividends were received by Neilson, but immediately turned over to Mr. Brooks. It was claimed that the $10,000 was a loan to Mr.

Neilson, but there was not the slightest evidence to sustain this point. When the stock of the Credit Mobilier, several months before this, had been increased fifty per cent., this was allotted to such of the stockholders as desired it *pro rata*, upon the payment of the par value thereof. Mr. Brooks claimed that, under the arrangement by which his stock came to him, that he or Neilson was entitled to an additional fifty shares of the Credit Mobilier stock. Finally, upon the principal stockholders signing an agreement to that effect, the fifty shares were transferred to him, and afterwards transferred to Neilson. Mr. Brooks was not only a member of Congress, but was a government director of the Union Pacific Railroad Company. As such it was his duty to watch over the interests of the government in the road and see that they were protected and preserved. The committee found that he had, through his official position, procured the stock of the Credit Mobilier, and bonds and stock of the Railroad, which he had no moral or legal right to obtain. And upon this finding they submitted a resolution for his expulsion from the House.

WILLIAM B. ALLISON, OF IOWA.

The committee in their report make no allusion to Mr. Allison, but in the testimony it appeared that he had several conversations with Mr. Ames, concerning Credit Mobilier stock, and finally received ten shares, on which no money was paid down. He received from Mr. Ames a memorandum, showing that the dividends had nearly paid the par value of the stock. In June, 1868, he received a dividend of $600, being by check on sergeant-at-arms. Mr. Allison at first stated that he had returned the stock and the dividends immediately upon their receipt by him, but he afterwards testfied that it was some time later. It appeared only on the cross examination of Mr. Ames that the stock had been returned after the investigation began, and was with the understanding that as soon as the matter had blown over, Mr. Ames was again to give him the stock, the consideration for the surrender to Mr. Ames being only nominal. The check had been cashed by Mr. Allison. Owing to his popularity and the influence of his friends the committee were prevailed upon to pass Mr. Allison by without mention.

JAMES A. GARFIELD, OF OHIO.

The Committee say: —

The facts in regard to Mr. Garfield, as found by the committee, are identical with the case of Mr. Kelley, to the point of reception of the check for $329. He agreed with Mr. Ames to take ten shares of Credit Mobilier stock, but did not pay for the same. Mr. Ames received the 80 per cent. dividend in bonds, and sold them for 97 per cent., and also received the 60 per cent. cash dividend, which together paid the price of the stock and interest, and left a balance of $329. This sum was paid over to Mr. Garfield by a check on the sergeant-at-arms, and Mr. Garfield then understood this sum was the balance of dividends after paying for the stock. Mr. Ames received all the subsequent dividends, and the committee do not find that, since the payment of the $329, there has been any communication between Mr. Ames and Mr. Garfield on the subject, until this investigation began. Some correspondence between Mr. Garfield and Mr. Ames, and some conversations between them during this investigation, will be found in the reported testimony.

The following is the statement of Gen. Garfield (Jan. 14, 1873):

The first time I ever heard of the Credit Mobilier was some time in 1866 or 1867—I cannot fix the date—when George Francis Train called on me and said he was organizing a company to be known as the Credit Mobilier of America, to be founded on the model of the Credit Mobilier of France; that the object of the company was to purchase lands and build houses along the line of the Pacific Railroad at points where cities and villages were likely to spring up; that he had no doubt money thus invested would double or treble itself each year; that subscriptions were limited to $1,000 each, and he wished me to subscribe. He showed me a long list of subscribers, among them Mr. Oakes Ames, to whom he referred me for further information concerning the enterprise. I answered that I had not the money to spare, and if I had I would not subscribe without knowing more about the proposed organization. Mr. Train left me, saying he would hold a place open for me, and hoped I would yet conclude to subscribe. The same day I asked Mr. Ames what he thought of the enterprise. He expressed the opinion that the investment would be safe and profitable.

I heard nothing further on the subject for a year or more, and it was almost forgotten, when some time, I should say, during the long session of 1868, Mr. Ames spoke of it again; said the company had organized, was doing well, and he thought would soon pay large dividends. He said some of the stock had been left, or was to be left, in his hands to sell, and I could take the amount which Mr. Train had offered me, by paying the $1000 and the accrued interest. He said if I was not able to pay for it then he would hold it for me till I could pay, or until some of the dividends were payable. I told him I would consider the matter; but would not agree to take any stock, until I knew, from an examination of the charter and the condition of the subscription, the extent to which I should become pecuniarily liable. He said he was not sure, but thought a stockholder would be liable only for the par value of his stock ; that he had not the stock and papers with him, but would have them after a while.

From the case, as presented, I probably should have taken the stock if I had been satisfied in regard to the extent of pecuniary liability. Thus the matter rested for some time, I think until the following year. During the interval I understood there were dividends due amounting to nearly three times the par value of the stock. But in the meantime I had heard that the company was involved in some controversy with the Pacific Railroad, and that Mr. Ames' right to sell the stock was denied. When I next saw Mr. Ames I told him I had concluded not to take the stock. There the matter ended, so far as I was concerned, and I had no further knowledge of the company's operations until the matter began to be discussed in the newspapers last fall. Nothing was ever said to me by Mr. Train, or Mr. Ames, to indicate or imply that the Credit Mobilier was, or could be, in any way connected with the legislation of Congress for the Pacific Railroad, or for any other purpose. Mr. Ames never gave, nor offered to give, any stock, or other valuable thing, as a gift. I once asked and obtained from him, and afterwards repaid to him, a loan of $300; that amount is the only valuable thing I ever received from, or delivered to him.

I never owned, received, or agreed to receive, any stock of the Credit Mobilier, or of the Union Pacific Railroad, nor any dividends or profits arising from either of them.

As the conversations and correspondence mentioned by the committee in their report are important to show the relation of the parties to the transaction, the testimony of Mr. Ames is here given in full.

By the CHAIRMAN:—

Q. In regard to Mr. Garfield, state to the committee the details of the transactions between you and him in reference to the Credit Mobilier stock.

A. I got for Mr. Garfield ten shares of the Credit Mobilier stock, for which he paid par and interest.

Q. When did you agree with him for that?

A. That agreement was in December, 1867, or January, 1868, about the time I had these conversations with all of them. It was all about the same time.

Q. State what grew out of it.

A. Mr. Garfield did not pay me any money. I sold the bonds belonging to his $1,000 of stock at 97, making $776. In June I received a dividend in cash on his stock of $600, which left a balance due him of $329, which I paid him. That is all the transaction between us. I did not deliver him any stock before or since. That is the only transaction, and the only thing.

By MR. MERRICK:—

Q. The $329 which you paid him was the surplus earnings on the stock above the amount to be paid for it, par value?

A. Yes, sir; he never had either his Credit Mobilier stock or Union Pacific Railroad stock. The only thing he realized on the transaction was the $329.

Q. I see by this statement of the account with General Garfield there is a charge of $47; that is interest from July previous, is it?

A. Yes. sir.

Q. And the $776 on the credit side of the account is the 80 per cent. bond dividend sold at 97?

A. Yes, sir.

Q. And the $600 on the credit side is the money dividend?

A. Yes, sir.

Q. And after you had received these two sums, they in the aggregate overpaid the price of the stock and interest $329, which you paid him?

A. Yes, sir.

Q. Did you make a statement of this to Mr. Garfield?

A. I presume so; I think I did with all of them; that is my impression.

Q. When you paid him this $329, did you understand it was the balance of his dividend after paying for the stock?

A. I suppose so. I do not know what else he could suppose.

Q. You did not deliver the certificate of stock to him?

A. No, sir; he said nothing about that.

Q. Why did he not receive his certificate?

A. I do not know.

Q. Do you remember any conversation between you and him in the adjustment of these accounts?

A. I do not.

Q. You understood that you were the holder of his ten shares?

A. Yes, sir.

Q. Did he so understand it?

A. I presume so. It seems to have gone from his mind, however.

Q. Was this the only dealing you had with him in reference to any stock?

A. I think so.

Q. Was it the only transaction of any kind?

A. The only transaction.

Q. Has that $329 ever been paid to you?

A. I have no recollection of it.

Q. Have you any belief that it ever has?

A. No, sir.

Q. Did you ever loan General Garfield $300?

A. Not to my knowledge; except that he calls this a loan.

Q. You do not call it a loan?

A. I did not at the time. I am willing it should go to suit him.

Q. What we want to get at is the exact truth.

A. I have told the truth in my statement.

Q. When you paid him $329, did he understand that he borrowed that money from you?

A. I do not suppose so.

Q. Have you any belief now that he supposed so?

A. No; only from what he said the other day. I do not dispute anybody.

Q. We want your judgment of the transaction.

A. My judgment of the transaction is just as I told you. There was but one thing about it.

Q. That amount has never been repaid you? You did not suppose that you had any right to it, or any claim to it.

A. No, sir.

Q. You regarded that as money belonging to him after the stock was paid for?
A. Yes, sir.
Q. There were dividends of Union Pacific Railroad stock on these ten shares?
A. Yes, sir.
Q. Did General Garfield ever receive these?
A. No, sir; never has received but $329.
Q. And that he received as his own money?
A. I suppose so; it did not belong to me. I should not have given it to him if it had not belonged to him.
Q. You did not understand it to belong to you as a loan; you never called for it, and have never received it back?
A. No, sir.
Q. Has there ever been any conversation between you and him in reference to the Pacific stock he was entitled to?
A. No, sir.
Q. Has he ever called for it?
A. No, sir.
Q. Have you ever offered it to him?
A. No, sir.
Q. Has there ever been any conversation in relation to it?
A. No, sir.
Q. Has there ever been anything said between you and him about rescinding the purchase of the ten shares of the Credit Mobilier stock? Has there anything been said to you of its being thrown up, or abandoned, or surrendered?
A. No, sir, not until recently.
Q. How recently?
A. Since this matter came up.

Q. Since this investigation commenced?
A. Yes, sir.
Q. Did you consider, at the commencement of this investigation, that you held these other dividends, which you say you did not pay to him, in his behalf? Did you regard yourself as custodian of these dividends for him?
A. Yes, sir; he paid for his stock, and is entitled to his dividends.
Q. Will the dividends come to him at any time on his demand?
A. Yes, sir, as soon as this suit is settled.
Q. You say that $329 was paid to him; how was it paid to him?
A. I presume by a check on the sergeant-at-arms. I find there are some checks filed without any letters or initials indicating who they were for.
Q. Have you had any correspondence, since this dividend was paid, with him, in regard to this matter?
A. I don't know what matter you refer to.
Q. If you had any correspondence I would like to see it.
A. I have no copy of it.
Q. Have you the original?
A. No, sir. Mr. Garfield showed me a letter which he said he intended to inclose with some money sent me. I did not know who the money came from. He showed me a letter which he said he intended to have put in. I indorsed on the back of that letter my reply. I just turned over the letter and wrote what I wrote on the back of it, and let him have it.
Q. Your answer, indorsed on the back of it, was published in the newspapers?
A. Yes, sir; he published the letter, I believe.
Q. As published did they correspond with your recollection of the papers as written?

A. Yes, sir. I wrote it off hastily. He came to my room, and said he had been accused of all kinds of crimes and misdemeanors. I told him I had made no such statements as he represented. He wanted me to say in writing that I had not. I took his letter which he said he intended to have inclosed with the money, and wrote on the back of it that I had made no such statement.

Q. The published correspondence in the morning papers of the next day is your recollection of what occurred?

A. It agrees with my recollection, except he says he left a letter for me at the Arlington. I never received that letter. I only saw the letter on which I indorsed my answer.

Q. Did he inclose the money?

A. Some money came to me inclosed in an envelope, which he said he had sent. I gave it back to him.

Q. How much money was in that envelope?

A. About four hundred dollars.

The following is a copy of the memorandum referred to by witness as a statement of his account with Mr. Garfield:

J. A. G.   DR.

1868.	To 10 shares stock Credit Mobilier of A.	$1000 00
	Interest	47 00
June 19.	To cash	329 00
		$1376 00

CR.

1868.	By dividend bonds Union Pacific Railroad, $1000 at 80 per cent. less 3 per cent.	$776 00
Jun. 17.	By dividend collected for your acc't	600 00
		$1376 00

Q. You may state whether, in conversation with you, Mr. Garfield claimed, as he claimed before us, that the only transaction between you was borrowing $300?

A. No, sir; he did not claim that with me.

Q. State how he does claim it with you; what was said. State all that occurred in conversation between you.

A. I can not remember half of it. I have had two or three interviews with Mr. Garfield. He wants to put it on the basis of a loan. He states that, when he came back from Europe, being in want of funds, he called on me to loan him a sum of money. He thought he had repaid it. I do not know. I cannot remember.

Q. What did you say to him in reference to that state of the case?

A. I stated to him that he never asked me to lend him any money; that I never knew he wanted to borrow any. I did not know he was short. I made a statement to him, showing the transaction, and what there was due on it; that, deducting the bond dividend and cash dividend, there was $329 due him, for which I had given him a check; that he had never asked me to loan him any money, and I never loaned him any.

Q. After you had made that statement, what did he state in reply?

A. He wanted to have it go as a loan.

Q. Did he claim that it was, in fact, a loan?

A. No, sir; I do not think he did. No; he did not.

Q. Go on, then, and state what was said — all the discussion that took place.

A. I cannot tell you all; we had three or four talks. I cannot remember what was said.

Q. How long after that transaction did he go to Europe?

A. I believe it was a year or two.

Q. Did you have any conversation in reference to the influence this transaction would have upon the election last fall?

A. Yes; he said it would be very injurious to him.

Q. What else in reference to that?

A. I am very bad to repeat conversation; I cannot remember.

Q. State all you know in reference to it.

A. I told him he knew very well that that was a dividend. I made out a statement, and showed it to him at the time. In one conversation he admitted it, and said, as near as I can remember, that there was $2,400 due him in stock and bonds. He made a little memorandum of $1,000 and $1,400, and, as I recollect, said there was $1,000 of Union Pacific Railroad stock, $1,000 of Credit Mobilier stock, and $400 of stock or bonds. I do not recollect what.

Q. When was that memorandum made?

A. It was made in my room; I cannot remember the date. It was since this investigation commenced.

Q. Was it in that conversation that he referred to the influence this matter would have upon the election in his district?

A. I do not recollect whether it was in that one or some other. I have had two or three conversations with him.

Q. Tell as nearly as you can, precisely the remarks he made in that connection.

A. It was that it would injure his reputation; that it was a cruel thing. He felt very bad, was in great distress, and hardly knew what he did say.

Q. Did he make any request of you to make no statement in reference to it?

A. I am not positive about that.

Q. What is your best recollection in reference to it?

A. My impression is that he wanted to say as little about it as he could, and to get off as easily as he could. That was about the conversation I had with him, about the long and short of it.

Q. Have you the memorandum that Mr. Garfield made?

A. I have the figures he made.

[Paper shown to committee, containing figures as follows :—]

$1,000
1,400
———
2,400

Q. You say those figures were made by Mr. Garfield?

A. Yes, sir.

Q. What do these sums represent? How did he put them down?

A. $1,000 Union Pacific Railroad stock; $1,000 Credit Mobilier stock, and $400, which he could not remember whether it was to be in cash, stock, or bonds.

Q. Is that what he received, or was entitled to?

A. What he was entitled to.

Q. That was his idea of what was coming to him?

A. Yes, sir.

Q. Was that about what he would have been entitled to?

A. He would have been entitled to the $1,000 in stock, and he would have been entitled to more than that. The $400 I think he is in error about. I gave him $329; I do not know whether the $400 referred to that.

Q. Did he put this down as his recollection of the statement you made to him?

A. I so understood it.

Q. It was in this conversation that these figures were made, that he deprecated the effect of the matter upon his election?

A. I do not know about his election; it was about his prospects, his reputation, &c.

Q. I understand that in substance he desired you to say as little as possible about it?

A. Yes, sir; and that is my desire.

Q. Will you repeat just what he did say.

A. I cannot remember the conversation well enough to repeat it.

Q. You can repeat the substance of it?

A. I have given you the substance of it.

Q. How did you happen to retain this little stray memorandum?

A. I do not know. I found it on my table two or three days afterward. I did not pay any attention to it, at the time, until I found there was to be a conflict of testimony, and I thought it might be something worth preserving.

Q. The conversation was in your room, and the figures were made there?

A. Yes, sir.

Q. Do I understand you that this loan which Mr. Garfield claims to have been made was in reference to a trip to Europe taken by him a year or two afterward?

A. I do not know when he took his trip. I know he did not go during that session of Congress. This payment was made to him during that session of 1867-'68.

Q. Do you know whether he went during that recess following?

A. I cannot say. I do not know.

Q. Do you know that he did not go to Europe for nearly two years afterward?

A. No; I do not. It is my impression it was two years afterward, but I cannot remember dates. People ask me about things that occurred a year ago, and I cannot tell whether it was ten years ago or one.

By the Chairman: —

Q. Did you understand in this conversation you had with General Garfield, that you detailed to him the history of this matter as to how the statement you had let him have was made up? and did you understand him to concede your statement about it to be the truth?

A. Well, I cannot say. He would not have been very apt to recollect the amount there was due him if he had not acceded to my statement.

Q. From the whole conversation — from what he said, and the figures that he made, did you understand him to concede the statement you had made to him as about the truth?

A. Yes; I so understood him.

Q. That statement you made to him was in substance the statement you made to us in reference to him?

A. Yes, sir.

JAMES W. PATTERSON OF NEW HAMPSHIRE.

Mr. Patterson purchased of Mr. Ames, August 31, 1867, thirty shares of the Credit Mobilier, paying therefor $3000, which stock he subsequently transferred to Morton, Bliss & Co., of New York, and later purchased $4,000 of stocks and bonds of the Union Pacific Railroad, which were sold for Mr. Patterson by Morton, Bliss & Co. From the Credit Mobilier stock Mr. Patterson received as dividends, February 14, 1868, $2,328; June 23, 1868, $1,800; May 6, 1871, $757.24 and 100 shares of Union Pacific stock, and $2,000 income bonds of that road. Mr. Patterson's testimony was to the effect that he gave to Mr. Ames $3,000 to invest for him, and that he was not aware, and in fact never knew, that he had purchased any Credit Mobilier stock with it; on the contrary, his impression had always been that the money had been invested by Mr. Ames in Union Pacific stock and bonds. But the committee (from the Senate) say:

> As a matter of fact, the committee find that the $3000 paid by Patterson to Ames was the purchase money of thirty shares of Credit Mobilier stock on the 31st of August, 1867, positive testimony of Mr. Ames to this effect, the payment of dividends in February following upon that amount of stock, and again in June, when he receipts to Ames "for $1800 on account of dividends received by him as trustee on stock for my account."

In May, 1871, an adjustment of matters is had between the parties, and Mr. Patterson gives Mr. Ames a receipt for "$757.24 in cash, on account of the transaction thirty shares of stock in the Credit Credit Mobilier stock, and there are still due in Mobilier of America, and $2,000 in income bonds of the Union Pacific Railroad."

Mr. Patterson says, in regard to these receipts, that Mr. Ames came to him some months after his giving the money to invest, and said, " I have sold your bonds," and paid to him some money, for which he gives a receipt, without giving any heed to the character of the receipt, and that the impression on his mind was, that Mr. Ames had disposed of securities in the road, and nothing connecting with the Credit Mobilier. The same committee, however, say in their report:

The committee find in the statement of Mr. Patterson before the committee of the House of **Representatives**, and his statement before this committee, a contradictory relation of the transaction between him and Mr. Ames; a suppression of material facts, and a denial of other facts which must have been known to him.

The committee then further review this transaction, and conclude their report as follows :

And further, that being inquired of in relation thereto before committees of both branches of Congress, he gave a false account of the transactions between himself and Mr. Ames, suppressed material facts, and denied the existence of other material facts which must have been well known to him.

The committee have reached a conclusion, after the most attentive consideration and anxious deliberation, which they would fain wish were otherwise, but a sense of duty compels them to declare.

They submit the following resolution :

Resolved, That James W. Patterson be, and he is hereby expelled from his seat as a member of the Senate.

No definite action was taken on this report, and five days after, the term of Mr. Patterson expired.

Mr. Patterson subsequently addressed the Senate in a long reply, vindicating his actions, but which we cannot insert here.

SCHUYLER COLFAX.

The committees from the House and from the Senate, in their reports, make no mention whatever of the name of Mr. Colfax, at that time Vice-President of the United States. But from the testimony that was taken before the House committee much of interest may be gleaned. January 7, 1868, he made the following statement before the committee :

I may add that Mr. Ames will recollect, when I call to mind the circumstances of the transaction, that he never paid me a dollar, or the value of a dollar, on any account whatever. * * I repeat that I never did receive a dollar, or the value of a dollar, on any account whatever, from him ; and I think Mr. Ames will recollect that I did not, when I recall to his mind these circumstances, which would of course impress themselves more on my mind than his, as it was a larger matter to me than to him. * * * * * * * * * * *

I state explicitly that no one ever gave, or offered to give me, any shares of stock in the Credit Mobilier, or the Union Pacific Railroad I have never received, or had tendered to me, any dividends in cash, stock, or bonds, accruing upon any stock in either of said organizations. And neither Mr. Ames, nor any other person connected with either of said organizations, ever asked me to vote for or against any measures affecting the interests of either, directly or remotely, or to use any personal or official influence in their favor. I desire, however, to state all the circumstances through which, probably, my name came to be associated with this organization.

Five years ago, about the time of the holiday recess, I was conversing on the floor of the House with Mr. Ames in regard to the Union Pacific Railroad, in favor of the building of which I had previously made hundreds of public addresses. In the course of this conversation he asked if I would not like to purchase some stock in the Credit Mobilier. Up to that time I knew nothing of its capital or profits ; and I enquired of him as to its objects and the value of its stock.

As near as I can recall this conversation, after the lapse of so many years, I was informed by him that it was a legally incorporated company, composed of the principal stockholders of the Union Pacific Railroad. who were themselves building the road, instead of letting it out to contractors who always expected large profits for their risks and for their advances of moneys for supplies. I told him, after his explanation, that it looked like a good and safe investment for one of limited means, and that I would be willing to purchase twenty or thirty shares at a fair price if I had the money. But I added frankly that I could not pay for them till two or three months afterward, as my housekeeping expenses in the opening months of the session were much larger than the average. He said he would contract to sell me twenty shares at par, if I would, in addition, agree to pay interest until final payment. I enquired what per cent. it would pay, and he replied that there had been large dividends, but as the road was pushed further into the interior the profits might not be large, though they would be very surely remunerative.

The Union Pacific Railroad had no legislation, that I knew of, pending before Congress at the time, nor did I suppose there could be any in the future, as the last amendment to their charter, authorizing the issue of first-mortgage bonds, which should have priority of the government lien, had been enacted in 1864, over three years before this conversation. Inferring that any questions arising under this charter would be judicially settled, and supposing, at any rate, that I had the same right to purchase this stock as to buy stock in a national bank chartered by Congress, or in a manufactory, I told him I would agree to purchase twenty shares at par, and interest, to be paid for as soon as I had the money. Some weeks, or months, afterward, at the same session, I paid Mr. Ames about $500 in cash on this contract of purchase, being all the money I had; but received no dividend or certificate, in whole or in part. My impression is that he told me that one or two dividends had been earned, but they were not in cash, and were as yet unadjusted. Certainly I did not receive any, and was not offered any in cash, bonds, or stock, then or since. A few weeks, or months, after this, I heard a rumor that unpleasant controversies existed among the largest stockholders, which were certain to involve the organization in prolonged litigation.

The very day I heard this rumor I told Mr. Ames that no profits, present or prospective, could induce me to buy into a lawsuit; that I had never been, during all my life, a plaintiff or a defendant in a court of justice; and that I must, therefore, recede entirely from the transaction between us, as I did not want stock of any kind, on any terms, that would make me a party to litigation. He assented to this, and nothing was said as to the money paid, my anxiety being not to get into a lawsuit. All these things occurred at the same session of Congress, five years ago, which closed in the summer of 1868. The next year, or the year after, Mr. Ames suspended payment, in consequence, as was said, of financial involvements connected with the Pacific Railroad, and his creditors gave him an extension on his liabilities. But, regretting his failure and its cause, I voluntarily told him to dismiss from his mind the small amount of money between us. I suppose, but for this, he would have repaid me the money I paid him. I may repeat, therefore, that neither stock nor bonds were given to me, nor offered to be given to me; that I have never received a dollar in bonds, stock, or money, as dividends; that I did contract to purchase twenty shares of stock n the company at par and interest, but that, after a partial payment. I withdrew entirely from what I regarded as an uncompleted contract to purchase, from repugnance to being involved in litigation; and that, instead of being enriched by it one thousand or twenty thousand dollars, as has been charged, I am voluntarily out of pocket five hundred dollars, and have been for nearly five years.

The testimony of Mr. Ames is that he secured for Mr. Colfax twenty shares of Credit Mobilier stock, which he "was to hold until paid for; that he received a dividend on them of eighty per cent. in bonds, which bonds he sold and accounted for to Mr. Colfax; which left a balance due on the stock of $534.72, which Mr. Colfax paid him with a check; the date of the check was March 5, 1868."

The following are the questions by Judge Polland, the chairman, with Mr. Ames' answers:

Q. Were there any dividends on that stock afterward?
A. There was one dividend. There were other dividends in stock which I never delivered to him. There was a dividend in cash, in June, which I did pay to him.

Q. How large was that?
A. Twelve hundred dollars.

Q. Have you any receipt or voucher for that?
A. No, sir; I gave him a check on the sergeant-at-arms, and it is charged to me there.

Q. And you got this date from the sergeant-at-arms' book?
A. Yes; I never delivered to Mr. Colfax anything else, and never received anything from him except that

time. He paid me for the balance of the stock, and I paid him a cash dividend.

* * * * * * * * * * *

Q. At the time you paid him $1,200, or gave him a check upon the sergeant-at-arms for that amount, did Mr. Colfax understand that this was a dividend on this Credit Mobilier stock?

A. I suppose so; I do not know; I so understood it. That is what it was; whether he understood the matter is more than I know; I do not know that I gave him any explanation. I gave him the check.

Q. Have you any doubt that you told him what it was?

A. I cannot remember. When I suppose a man knows a thing I don't tell him over again.

Q. Do you remember whether he made any inquiry as to what it was?

A. I don't remember anything about what was said at all.

Q. You supposed that it was understood that it was a dividend you had received upon that stock?

A. I supposed so.

Q. Has he ever repaid you that $1,200?

A. Not to my knowledge. It did not belong to me.

Q. You never made any claim upon him for it, and did not suppose you had any right to it.

A. No, sir.

Q. These $534 that were paid you, you did not suppose he had any right to call upon you to pay back?

A. I did not suppose so; I understood that I sold him $2,000 worth of stock. The first dividend, 80 per cent. in bonds, and that check for $534, paid for the stock. That was my supposition.

By Mr. Merrick: —

Q. In what order of time were the two dividends paid, of $1,200 and $500?

A. He paid me $500 in March, and I paid him $1,200 in the June following.

Q. Were there any other different transactions between you and Mr. Colfax to which these payments could refer at all, except this Credit Mobilier?

A. No, sir.

Q. What memoranda or entries have you in reference to this transaction?

A. I made a little memorandum at the time, I suppose, which I handed him; when, I don't remember.

Q. Have you any memorandum with you?

A. No, sir.

Q. Have you made a memorandum of it at all?

A. Yes; I took a copy of the memorandum I made, and brought it with me. When I went home, you asked me to look over my books. I did, and found I had received $534 from Mr. Colfax, and I found I had charged him with $1,200 in June.

Q. Have you the memorandum made at the time?

A. No, sir; not here; I have a memorandum which I took from that.

Q. What was the character of the book in which the memorandum was made?

A. It was a small pocket memorandum, and some of it on slips of paper.

Q. It was entered in journal form?

A. No; it was simply a small memorandum book. These things were closed up at the time here, and they were not entered on my books at home.

Q. Is what you have here a copy of your memorandum made at the time?

A. Yes, sir; that contains the names I took from my books.

Q. The only entry in this in reference to Mr. Colfax is the $534. The $1,200 was not put on this memorandum?

A. No, sir.

By the CHAIRMAN:—

Q. Both these entries were made in this book, the $500 to pay the balance of the stock, and the $1.200 which were paid in June by a check on the sergeant-at-arms?

A. Yes; they were both on that book. I have looked it over to see, and I have looked over the sergeant-at-arms' book to see if my entries were correct, and I find they are.

By MR. MCCRARY:—

Q. Did Mr. Colfax tell you at any time that he had concluded not to take the stock?

A. I have no recollection of it, unless it was in that conversation to which he has referred. I have no recollection of it.

Q. Have you any recollection of informing him of the litigation that had sprung up in regard to it?

A. I think I did; I think I told them all.

Q. You do not remember what he said when you informed him of that?

A. No, sir.

Q. Did you not understand that this sale of stock to Mr. Colfax was rescinded; that the trade was given up, and that he relinquished the stock to you?

A. Not unless he meant to be understood so in the conversation when I came back. I did not consider it given up. I did not consider that I had any right to withhold it.

Q. Was there any thing of the kind said between you?

A. I cannot recollect; it might have been said; but I cannot recollect it.

Q. Have you ever been reimbursed for that $1,200?

A. No, sir.

At this point in Mr. Ames' testimony, Mr. Colfax, with the permission of the committee, began to interrogate the witness. Many of the questions of little bearing are here omitted; but what are presented include all that are of importance.

Q. Now, when I testified on the 7th of January, and asked you to cross-examine me, if the statement I made was not correct, why did you not contradict me then?

A. I had not examined the records then; I had not refreshed my recollection.

Q. The subject had been discussed all over the country, and your attention must have been called to it.

A. My minutes were at home, and I had not examined them until I went back home.

Q. You say you paid me $1,200 by a check on the sergeant-at-arms?

A. I did.

Q. Where was I when you paid me?

A. I do not know; I cannot say. The check is in the sergeant-at-arms' room.

Q. Now, when I asserted, in my testimony, that I had never received a dollar from you, why did you not contradict me then, and say to the committee that you had paid me a check of $1,200?

A. I was not in a position to contradict you, because I had not examined my minutes, and refreshed my recollection.

Q. Did I not tell you the first of the present session that I wanted you to tell the whole truth about the matter?

A. Well, I think I have done so.

Q. Why not have done so at first? Why didn't you tell it when I was here and gave my testimony? Why didn't you state that you had paid me $1,200?

A. I did not want to dispute you.

Q. You say that was the only cash dividend in 1868 upon this stock?

A. I think the only cash dividend.

Q. In Mr. Durant's testimony there is a statement that there was a cash dividend of 30 per cent. in July, 1868?

A. I think not.

Q. Mr. Durant also states that there was a bond dividend during that session. What did you do with the bonds belonging to me?

A. There are bonds belonging to you now.

Q. You did not sell all the bonds then?

A. No; there are bonds that belong to you now, bonds that belong to your stock, and that you are entitled to.

Q. Where is what I am entitled to now?

A. I hold it.

Q. Have you ever offered it to me?

A. No, sir; I am waiting for the result of this suit.

Q. Have you ever told me any thing about it?

A. I suppose I told you about it in 1868, when I told several others.

Q. You do not think you told me, do you?

A. I do not know whether I did; I suppose I gave you a statement.

Q. Now, in regard to this thing being off, you say you got that from my testimony?

A. It must have been from a conversation with you since we have been here this present session. I called upon you at your room.

Q. Did you have any other checks on the sergeant-at-arms at the same time that you gave me this one for $1,200?

A. Yes, sir.

Q. You do not remember when you paid me this $1,200 check?

A. I suppose it was in the House. The sergeant-at-arms paid it.

Q. Was it paid to my order?

A. It was payable to "S. C. or bearer."

Q. Paid to me by the sergeant-at-arms?

A. I think so. It is in his possession as a voucher for the money, and my books show that I gave you the check at the time for $1,200.

Q. Is it not more probable that you got the money on that check yourself, as we had this talk about being off?

A. That check was given a long while before I had any talk about being off. This check was given in June, 1868.

Q. My recollection is that the talk we had about being off was in the summer of 1868, at the same session at which you say the check was given.

A. There had been no litigation then.

Q. Was it not in regard to prospective litigation that we were talking?

A. No; I did not know anything about any litigation or suit until after June.

Q. You are positive that you paid me this check for $1,200?

A. I am positive I gave you the check.

Q. And then I ask you again, why did you not say so when you testified in December?

A. I testified that I had paid you the dividends.

Q. You stated in your first examination that you could not remember having paid me any dividends. Then, in your cross-examination, you said that possibly you might have paid me, but you were not certain.

A. Yes; now I am certain.

Q. Then this transaction had passed out of your mind, so that you were not certain then?

A. I could not remember the amount at all until I had examined my books. I examined my books when I went home, and when I returned to Washington I compared my memorandums with the checks the sergeant-at-arms has on file, and I found my check filled out " S. C. ", which corresponded with the memorandum I had on my book.

Mr. Colfax again said:

I want again to state to the committee, as I before stated, that I do not remember ever having received one dollar from Mr. Ames, and I hope to be able to prove that fact. I think there is a mistake in the statement Mr. Ames makes.

The following is the memorandum from which Mr. Ames testified in relation to Mr. Colfax:

S. C. Dr.			Cr.	
1868.			1868.	
To 20 shares stock C. M. of A.	$2,000	00	March 5. By cash	$534 72
To interest . . .	86	72	Feb. 14. Dividends of bonds U. P. R. R., $2,000 80; $1,600, less 3 per cent . .	1,552 00
June 19. To cash	1,200	00	June 17. By dividend collected for his account	1,200 00
	$3,286	72		$3,286 72

The following day considerable testimony was given, both by Mr. Ames and Mr. Colfax, each maintaining strongly the positions taken above, Mr. Ames asserting positively that he paid Mr. Colfax the $1,200, and accounted to him for the other dividends, and producing the check of $1,200. Mr. Colfax as positively denied its receipt, but said that he understood that the $534.72 which he paid Mr. Ames was to pay in full for the stock in connection with the unadjusted dividends of which Mr. Ames made mention.

Mr. Colfax also made the following statement:

I wish to repeat exactly what I stated day before yesterday; that I never received from Mr. Ames a dollar on any account whatsoever. I never saw this check. I never knew, until I saw this check this morning, whether Mr. Ames signed his name O. Ames or Oakes Ames. Why, if the check was for me, he should have filled it out with "S. C. or bearer," I cannot imagine. If I had seen a check so filled out, it would have struck me very forcibly. Now I could not have had $1,200 added to my income without remembering it very positively. I could not have talked with Mr. Ames afterwards about sympathizing with him in his misfortunes, and proposed to remit to him the $500 I had paid him, if I had received $1,200 from him.

The sergeant-at-arms and assistants testified that the various checks were paid, some with only initials, and some with whole names; that a check payable to initials or bearer would be paid without endorsement; but they could not tell to whom it was paid.

January 28, 1868, the cashier of the First National Bank of Washington, where Mr. Colfax had his account, was called, and testified as follows:

By the CHAIRMAN—

Q. Will you state, from the ledger which is open before you, whether it appears that Mr. Colfax made a deposit on the 22d of June, 1868?

A. It does.

Q. What is the amount?

A. By reference to the books I find it was $1,968.63.

Q. From that entry you understand that amount of money was deposited to his credit either by him or by somebody for him?

A. Yes, sir.

Q. State the various deposits made to his credit from that time during the month of July?

A. July 7, $400; July 8, $150; July 13, $1,543.87.

By MR. AMES:

Q. Can you state whether the deposit of the 22d June was in money or in checks?

A. It is entered as "cash items." It may have been money; it may have been checks.

By the CHAIRMAN:

Q. Have you the deposit check with you? If so, you will please read it.

A. It reads: "Deposited in the First National Bank by Schuyler Colfax, June 22, 1868.

United States and bank notes	$1,200	00
Checks as follows	250	00
	18	63
	500	00
	$1,968	63"

Q. You will look at your ledger and see when the last deposit of Mr. Colfax was made prior to the 22d June.

A. That was June 1st.

On the 6th of February Mr. Ames, at the request of the committee, produced his memorandum book, which is now so famous. The book was a small one, which Mr. Ames carried in his pocket, and used for the purpose of making private memoranda. When called upon by the committee to produce it, he did so, but desired that it should be exhibited only as to those matters before the committee. We shall not attempt to put in the different questions and answers relating to it, but shall give copies of the memoranda and explanation sufficient to make them clearly understood.

The first entry exhibited was that of Mr. Wilson, as follows: —

1868.
Tuesday, January 14.

Henry Wilson, cr. for cash on act. of C. M. of A. 70 00

1868. Monday, February 10.
For $1,600 bonds.

Paid H. Wilson 548 00
In Scofield check 195 33
U. P. R. R. check 308 72
Sergt.-at-Arms 44 00
                              ─────
                              548 05

Mr. Ames stated that there were several other business matters relating to Mr. Wilson upon the book which in no way related to the Credit Mobilier. This memorandum relates to the dividend of $1,600 in bonds on the 20 shares of Credit Mobilier which Mr. Wilson held.

The next entry relating to Mr. Wilson is as follows: —

1868.   Monday, June 22, 1868.
Hon. Henry Wilson.
By div. from U. P. R. R. $1,200
Cash 223 00
1 C. R. & M. R. bd. 950 00
Int'st from Feb. 1 . . . . 27 00   1,200

Bond to be ded.
Check on Bk. of Commerce 223

1868.   Saturday, January 11.
Rec'd of Hon. H. L. Dawes
Cash on acct. of stock in C.
M. of A.
$800, Jan'y 11.
235, " 14, ... $1,035.

This entry shows the payments for the stock as made, it being the par value of ten shares and interest.

Then next comes a statement of the different individuals entitled to receive dividends, and the amount. This book, which has the dates printed in it, runs over into the next year a day or two, and the following entries were made without any reference to the date, being simply a memorandum showing the amount of dividend due to each of the several holders of the bonds.

1868.   Saturday, January 1869.

H. L. Dawes	X 600 00
Scofield	X 600 00
Patterson	X 1,800 00
Painter	X 1,800 00
Wilson	X 1,200 00
Colfax	X 1,200 00
Bingham	X 1,200 00
Allison	X 600 00
Kelley	X 329 00
Wilson	X 329 00
Garfield	X 329 00

When the amount had been paid, Mr. Ames made the cross to show that fact. They relate to the cash dividend in June, 1868, and show simply the amount to be paid each.

The next entry is : —

1868.   Thursday, March 5.
Rec'd of Schuyler Colfax check balance . . . 534 72

The next entry regarding Mr. Colfax is a general statement such as was made in each case.

Colfax.

20 shares Credit Mobilier cost	$2,000 00
7 mos. 10 days' int'st	86 72
	2,086 72
Less 80 pr. ct. bds. at 97	1,552 00
Paid March 5	534 72

2,000 U. P. stock.
2,000 C. M. stock.

This entry was made previous to June, and does not include the dividend of $1,200 cash at that time, but shows the amount which Mr. Colfax paid to balance the cost of stock.

There were no other entries on the book regarding Mr. Colfax, except the payment of the $1,200, which entry occurs as follows : —

1868.   Sunday, June 31.

Checks on Commerce, deposited with
sergeant-at-arms	$10,000 00
Pd. S. Colfax	1,200 00
" James F. Wilson	329 00
" H. L. Dawes	600
" William B. Allison	600
" G. W. Scofield	600
" J. W. Patterson	1,800
" John A. Logan	329
" James A. Garfield	329
" William D. Kelley	329
" Henry Wilson	1,200
" John A. Bingham	1,200

Although the date would show it was made on Sunday, the remark made above that these simple memoranda were made on such blank pages as were convenient, applies here also. The $10,000 Mr. Ames deposited for the express purpose of paying these dividends from, and as they were adjusted he drew a check on the sergeant-at-arms for the amount, and the same was paid when presented.

Mr. Ames here produced his memorandum book for the year 1869, upon which there appeared one entry regarding Mr. Colfax, as follows : —

Friday, January 29, 1869.

Paid S. Colfax $60.75 for interest on $1500 certificate of U. P. R. R.

This entry was made and the amount paid, as Mr. Ames testified, on the day above. Mr. Colfax being entitled to interest on $1,500, the same as if the bonds themselves had been actually divided. He collected the interest, and paid the same to Mr. Colfax.

The next memorandum was as follows : —

1868   Wednesday, January 28.

Rec'd of Glenni W. Scofield check
on sergeant-of-arms 708 50
10 coupons, 350 East 350 00
Less 5 p'r c't 17 50
                                             332 50
                                             1,041 00

to be invested in 10 shares of Credit Mobilier of America, as trustee, by me, No. 346.

Immediately below this was the following entry : —

Feb'y 1st, 1868. — Del'd to Hon. Glenni W. Scofield certificate No. 346, for 10 shares of stock on Credit Mobilier, bot. for his account.

The next entry is —

1868.   Sunday, February 9.

Reached Washington from N. Y.

Del'd Glenni W. Scofield one bond . . 1,000
10 shares Stock 1,000
Rec'd of G. W. Scofield for balance due on his bond over his div., 195.33, & endorsed the same on my receipt.

The bond was worth eighty, which Mr. Scofield took, paying the balance in cash.

Then came the entry of the payment of the $600 cash dividend, as above, and in the back of the book, as follows : —

G. W. SCOFIELD.

By cash 1,041
On bond 195 33
                                    1,236 33
D'l'd him one bond. 1,000
                                    236 33
1,000 Credit.
1,000 U. P. R. R'd.

This entry, as it appeared upon Mr. Ames' memorandum book, is crossed out, showing it was closed, and that the whole transaction was ended.

The next entry is,

1868.   FRIDAY, April 24.
Rec'd of Wm. B. Allison 271 00
for balance due on stock sold him, 1,000 in Credit Mobilier, and 1,000 in Union Pacific R. road.

This amount is what would be due after the eighty per cent. dividend had been credited on this stock. This amount being paid by Mr. Allison, and therefore not deducted from the cash dividend of $600 in June.

The general statement is as follows:—

WM. B. ALLISON.

Ten shares Credit M	1,000
Interest to May	46
	1,046
Dividend in Bonds 80 pr. ct., sold at 97	776
Cash to balance	270

1,000 C. M.
1,000 U. P.

This being crossed off, **shows** that the account was finally closed.

The next is:—

JAMES F. WILSON.

10 shares C. M.	1,000	
7 mo. 10 days	43	36
	1,043	36
80 pr. cent. Div. at 97	776	
	267	36
Int's't to June 20	3	64
	271	00

1,000 U. P.
1,000 C. M.

This also was crossed off, showing it was finally closed.

Then follows:—

       1868.   FRIDAY, February 14.

Paid J. W. Patterson for 2,400$ bonds of Union
   Pacific R. R. Co. as dividend, less 3 pr. ct. . . . $2,328
      Less interest paid. 105

P'd Cash $2,223
Per receipt

And at the end of the book the general statement: —

Rec'd of J. W. Patterson
  Cash and Interest 3,105 00
  Rec'd for 3 Bonds   2,328
                                        ─────────
                                        5,433 00
  Feb'y 14 to Cash   2,328
                                        ─────────
                                        3,105 00
  3000 U. P. Stock
  3000 C. M. A. "

The next is the general statement of

JOHN A. BINGHAM.

  by Cash 2,086 72
  " Note 399 32
  to bonds . . 2,000
  Stock . . 2,000
  C. M . . 2,000

Mr. Bingham, it will be remembered, admitted that he took two bonds, paid par, and had the benefit of them.

Then comes the general statement of

WM. D. KELLEY

  10 shares C. M. A.   1,000
  7 mos. 10 days' int'st 43 36
                                        ─────────
                                        1,043 36
  80 pr. ct. bond div. at 97   776
                                        ─────────
                                         267 36
  Int'st to June 20 . . . .   3 64
                                        ─────────
                                         271

1,000 U. P. stock
1,000 C. M.

This statement was made just previous to the $600 cash dividend, which, credited to his account, leaves the balance due him $329, which Mr. Ames paid by check on the sergeant-at-arms. This account is not crossed off, as Mr. Ames had not yet delivered him the stock to which he was entitled.

There is one other item on this account:—

1868. TUESDAY, September 29.

William D. Kelley on com $750

This is the amount received later by Mr. Kelley, regarding which there was a dispute between them.

In regard to the next memorandum, that of Mr. Garfield, we wish to give the evidence.

By the CHAIRMAN:

Q. Now turn to any entries you may have in reference to Mr. Garfield.

A. Mr. Garfield's payments were just the same as Mr. Kelley's.

Q. I find Mr. Kelley's name on the list of June dividend payments for $329. That, I understand you, to be the amount of the June dividend, after paying the balance due on his stock?

A. Yes, sir; the general statement made up for Mr. Garfield is as follows:

GARFIELD

10 shares Credit M	1,000	
7 mos. 10 days	43	36
	1,043	36
80 per ct. bd. div. at 97	776	
	267	36

```
                                    267 36
Int'st to June 20  . . . . . . . . .  3 64
                                    ------
                                    271 00
```

1,000 C. M.
1,000 U. P.

Q. You received $600 cash dividend on his ten shares?
A Yes, sir.
Q And, as you say, paid him $329, as the balance of the dividend due him?
A. Yes, sir.
Q. The general statement is not crossed off?
A. No, sir.
Q. In the list of names for the June dividend, Mr. Garfield's name is down for $329?
A. That would be the balance due.
Q. The cross opposite his name indicates that the money was paid to him?
A. Yes, sir.

MR. CLARK remarked that Mr. Ames was not certain whether this amount was paid Mr. Garfield by check or in currency.

The WITNESS. If I drew the check I may have paid him off in currency, as I find no check with initials corresponding to his.

Q. We find three checks for the amount of $329 each; one is in blank; there are no initials written in. There are, however, the same number of checks for that amount as are called for by the names on this list for that amount.
A. I am not sure how I paid Mr. Garfield; I paid him in some form.
Q. This statement of Mr. Garfield's account is not crossed off, which indicates, does it, that the matter has never been settled or adjusted?
A. No, sir; it never has.

Next follows the general statement of

LOGAN.

10 shares C. M. A.	1,000	
7 mo. 10 days	43	36
	1,043	36
80 pr. ct. Div. at 97	776	
	267	36
Int'st to June 20.	3	64
	271	00

1,000 U. P.
1,000 C. M.

This general statement, like all the others, was made prior to the June dividend of $600 cash, and when that dividend was made there was a balance due Mr. Logan of $329, which he admits having received. The account was crossed off, showing all matters had been adjusted.

Here is the general statement of

HENRY WILSON.

Rec'd of him	1,000
two bonds 1,600	
Less 3 p'r cent	1,552
Cash	70
	2,622
p'd cash & Interest	1,548
	1,074

2,000 Credit
2,000 U. P. Stock

This account, having been finally settled, was crossed off, as were others.

This includes all the memoranda relating to members of Congress, as appearing upon his book.

Upon the conclusion of Mr. Ames' testimony regarding the memorandum book, he was cross-examined at great length by Mr. Robert S. Hale, who appeared in behalf of Mr. Colfax, but no new feature was brought out, nor were the former statements of Mr. Ames in the least shaken; on the contrary, his testimony was more positive. On the 11th February, 1873, Mr. Colfax again took the witness stand, at his own instance, and made a long statement, denying again, positively, the receipt of any money, or dividends, from Mr. Ames. In regard to the deposit of $1,200 in bills in his bank immediately after the time which the check of Mr. Ames was given and paid by the sergeant-at-arms, Mr. Colfax attempts to explain, by saying that $200 on the 11th of July, another letter came from Mr. of that amount he received in the month of June from his step-father, Mr. Matthews, on account of a debt which he owed him, and then says:

About the time of this payment, and, as near as I can fix the date, about the middle of the month of June, and very soon after the payment by Mr. Matthews, I was opening my letter-mail at the breakfast table, in accordance with my usual custom; and found an envelope within another envelope postmarked New York. On opening the inner envelope, I found it contained a letter written by George F. Nesbitt, congratulating me most cordially and warmly on my nomination for the Vice-Presidency, and saying that the writer desired to send me, confidentially, the remittance enclosed to aid me in the heavy expenses of the canvass, but wished it kept a secret, as neither his family nor any one else would ever know of it unless I told them. Inclosed in this letter was a greenback, or national bank bill, for $1,000.

He goes on, then, to say how he showed it to all his family, and speaks of the surprise that all exhibited as it passed around to each, and says he is sure he deposited it with the $200 received from Mr. Matthews. According to this, the deposit could not have been made within a week from the time of its receipt. This letter, containing such warm congratulations, had been lost, and he was unable to produce it before the committee. Further cross-examination brought out the fact that on the 18th of April, 1868, Mr. Colfax had received from this same Mr. Nesbitt a letter containing a *check* for $1,000, as a political contribution, and that again, on the 11th of July, another letter from Mr. Nesbitt, enclosing another *check* for $1,000, as a political contribution. Both of the letters containing these remittances, which were both in checks, Mr. Colfax produced before the committee. There was also another contribution of $1,000 from Mr. Nesbitt in November, at the end of the campaign. It may only be necessary to add that at this time Mr. Nesbitt held a contract from the Post Office Department for supplying envelopes, and Mr. Colfax was chairman of the Post Office Committee during a considerable portion of the continuance of this contract.

Such, in brief, is the testimony which the Polland Committee obtained from the various witnesses who appeared before them; but all that is of principal importance is herein contained. It then fell to the province of the committee to make up from this mass of testimony the report which they submitted to Congress. It would be impossible, in a work of this nature, to set that report out in full, and we must content ourselves with a brief summary. In the testimony which precedes, we have taken the report of the committee as the true statement of that evidence, except where we differ from that report, and where it became necessary to account for the difference of opinion we entertain regarding it.

The committee say that in December, 1867, after Mr. Ames came to attend the regular session of Congress, then opened, he made arrangements with certain members of Congress to take stock in the Credit Mobilier, and that he sold it to them at par and accrued interest from the July previous, while, in fact, the stock at that time was of far greater value, and was finding a ready sale at prices varying from $160 to $225 per share; that Mr. Ames, in selling at this price, did so for the purpose of creating such an interest in the recipients that their actions on any matter to be brought before Congress, affecting the Union Pacific Railroad, would be influenced in favor of the road, and to this extent must be considered a bribe; and they found that this was the object of Mr. Ames. To follow the language of the report:—

The committee do not find that Mr. Ames, in his negotiations with the persons above named, entered into any detail of the relations between the Credit Mobilier Company and the Union Pacific Company, or gave them any specific information as to the amount of dividends they would be likely to receive.

And again:—

The Credit Mobilier Company was a state corporation not subject to Congressional legislation, and the fact that its profits were to be derived from the building of the Union Pacific Railroad did not apparently create such an interest in that company as to disqualify the holder of Credit Mobilier stock from participating in any legislation affecting the railroad. In his negotiations with these members of Congress Mr. Ames made no suggestion that he desired to secure their favorable influence in Congress in favor of the railroad company, and whenever the question was raised as to whether the ownership of this stock would in any way interfere with, or embarrass them in, their action as members of Congress, he assured them it would not.

And again:—

The committee have not been able to find that any of these members of Congress have been affected in their official action in consequence of their interest in Credit Mobilier stock.

But the report goes on:—

The committee are also satisfied that Mr. Ames entertained a fear that, when the true relations between the Credit Mobilier Company and the Union Pacific became generally known, and the means by which the great profits expected to be made were fully understood, there was danger that Congressional investigation and action would be invoked.

The members of Congress with whom he dealt were generally those who had been friendly and favorable to a Pacific Railroad, and Mr. Ames did not fear, or expect to find them favorable to movements hostile to it; but he desired to stimulate their activity and watchfulness in opposition to any unfavorable action by giving them a personal interest in the success of the enterprise, especially so far as it affected the interest of the Credit Mobilier Company. On the 9th day of December, 1867, Mr. C. C. Washburn, of Wisconsin, introduced in the House a bill to regulate by law the rates of transportation over the Pacific Railroad.

Mr. Ames, as well as others interested in the Union Pacific road, was opposed to this, and desired to defeat it. Other measures, apparently hostile to that company, were subsequently introduced into the House by Mr. Washburn, of Wisconsin, and Mr. Washburne, of Illinois. The Committee believe that Mr. Ames, in his distributions of stock, had specially in mind the hostile efforts of the Messrs. Washburn, and desired to gain strength to secure their defeat. The reference in one of his letters to " Washburne's move" makes this quite apparent.

The committee also set out the transactions of Mr. Ames with the several members of Congress substantially as above, and after reflecting severely upon his conduct, concluded with the following resolulution :

1. *Whereas*, Mr. OAKES AMES, a Representative in this House, from the State of Massachusetts, has been

guilty of selling to members of Congress shares of stock in the Credit Mobilier of America, for prices much below the true value of such stock, with intent thereby to influence the votes and decisions of such members in matters to be brought before Congress for action: Therefore

Resolved, That Mr. OAKES AMES be, and he is hereby, expelled from his seat as a member of this House.

2. *Whereas* Mr. JAMES BROOKS, a Representative in this House from the State of New York, did procure the Credit Mobilier Company to issue and deliver to Charles H. Neilson, for the use and benefit of said BROOKS, fifty shares of the stock of said company, at a price much below its real value, well knowing that the same was so issued and delivered with intent to influence the votes and decisions of said BROOKS as a member of the House in matters to be brought before Congress for action, and also to influence the action of said BROOKS as a government director in the Union Pacific Railroad Company: Therefore,

Resolved, That Mr. JAMES BROOKS be, and he is hereby, expelled from his seat as a member in this House.

There are a few observations which it may be necessary to speak of. It was by no means settled by the testimony whether Mr. Ames solicited these members of Congress to take the stock, or whether they came to him first. It certainly was uncontradicted that in some cases these members came to him in regard to other investments, and when he recommended the Credit Mobilier, and gave them references concerning it, they took the pains to investigate, and then said they would purchase the stock. The whole evidence shows it to have been as any regular business transaction. The stock which Mr. Ames sold to members of Congress was his own, which he had paid for to the Credit Mobilier Company, at par. The question as to the time of these contracts for the sale of this stock has indeed a very important bearing in ascertaining the value of the stock which was sold by Mr. Ames. There was no conflict in the testimony of any of the many witnesses, that it was immediately after the opening of Congress in the winter of 1867-68, that all these conversations were had between Mr. Ames and those who purchased or who were approached by him regarding this stock. Five years had passed before this investigation began, and facts and dates might easily pass from memory. In the year 1867 there was an adjourned session of Congress, which met in the month of November, and continued in session day after day until the regular session opened on the second day of December. The two sessions ran into each other, the one being closed and the other immediately opened. When this adjourned session opened, and for nearly six weeks thereafter, the stock of the Credit Mobilier was offered for sale freely at par, with no buyers, and a sale was only occasionally made, and at less than par. Yet here is a fact, important in its bearings as it is, that was entirely overlooked by all the witnesses who testified, and especially by Mr. Ames, to whom it was so important. Search may be made through the entire testimony of every witness, without finding any mention of it whatever. Yet, as we said before, there was no conflict in the testimony of all the witnesses, that all these sales, or contracts, were agreed upon immediately after the assembling of Congress. It must, therefore, have been in the month of November, or the early days of December, at a time prior to the declaration of any dividends on Credit Mobilier stock, prior to any increase in its value, and at a time when it was a most difficult matter to dispose of the stock to any one at so high a price as par. It needed, therefore, the earnest solicitation of Mr. Ames to induce members to buy. .He assured them that the stock would be a good paying investment; but there was not a particle of evidence showing what the dividends might be;—nor was any statement made, because, at the time the contracts for the sales were made, it was not known that any dividend would be declared for some time in the future. The value of the stock was entirely speculative, and those who bought, or agreed to buy, did so as an investment, the same as any other man would do under similar circumstances. There were violent objections made to declaring these first dividends, and the first one was declared on the 12th of December, 1867. It was not until some time after this that the value of the stock began to rise. It was after this that Mr. Ames made his request to have shares of the stock issued him by the Credit Mobilier Company, in order that he might fulfil the obligations he had incurred. His agreement was that this stock should be delivered at par and interest from the July previous, and though the price in the meantime had greatly increased, still his word was as binding to him as his bond. He delivered the stock as he had agreed, though it was then far above the price he received. But, to be accurate, he did not *deliver* it, but held it in trust for those parties who had agreed to purchase. And why did he do this? The answer is plain. Had he given the stock to each buyer, and had that transfer recorded on the books of the Credit Mobilier, the holder would not have been entitled to any dividends, unless, being also a holder of Union Pacific stock, he had given his irrevocable proxy to the trustees. But while the stock remained in the name of Mr. Ames on the books of the Credit Mobilier, it would be entitled to its dividends when any should be declared. And for this reason no other transfer of the stock was made, and Mr. Ames merely made a memorandum on his private book regarding it, and without any pretense of system. Mr. Ames was not a bookkeeper; and in all those extraordinary transactions of business in which he was daily engaged, he carried the details in his head, trusting and relying upon his memory for all the accuracy he desired, and he never made an error.

There can be no manner of question but that Mr. Ames sold this stock, and that certain members of Congress purchased it, for this was admitted by all; whether a certain few who positively denied it made investments, is another question. Henry Wilson, John A. Logan, Henry L. Dawes, Glenni W. Scofield, John A. Bingham, B. F. Boyer, William B. Allison, James F. Wilson — all admitted that they bought it, and a portion of them returned it, while another portion of them retained it. There is no conflict in the testimony of these men, (unless it was in that of Mr. Allison), and that of Mr. Ames. In relation to James A. Garfield and Schuyler Colfax, the very same testimony applied to them that applied to the others — the same chain of circumstances connected them all. No question can remain in the mind of any who will read the statements of the parties, and the testimony and evidence, but that these two were untruthful, — that their statements and explanations were wholly and absolutely false from beginning to end, and that Mr. Ames told only the truth, and that his record of sales was true. Mr. Garfield having made his statement, and being confronted by the statements and evidence produced by Mr. Ames, which proved beyond all doubt in the mind of any one that the oath of Mr. Garfield was false, remained quiet and never opened his mouth to offer an explanation, to ask a question, or deny an assertion made by Mr. Ames. He had expected, after making his statement, that Mr. Ames would corroborate it, and thus place him before the world as clean and pure; but, when he found that Mr. Ames would tell the truth, he was wise enough to see that any controversy with Mr. Ames on this point would consign him to a political grave. He therefore remained silent. Not so with poor Colfax. He tried to break down the testimony of Mr. Ames, and each step only involved him deeper and deeper in falsehood. Every move he made only cast still stronger upon him the conviction of the entire nation that he was false, and that Mr. Ames was telling the truth.

A word or two as to the findings of the committee. They could not find that Mr. Ames had used any persuasion to get congressmen to buy the stock, or that he had made any particular representation as to its value, or the dividends to be expected. They could not find that the holding of this stock would create such an interest as to disqualify the holder in participating in any legislation affecting the Pacific road; and they found, as a fact, that none of them had been influenced, in their legislative actions, in consequence of their holding the stock.

But in spite of this, in view even of the fact that the possession of such would not and did not create any unlawful interest, the committee were of the opinion that Mr. Ames had sold it to them with that purpose in view, and that he intended to do that which the committee found could not be done, therefore, as it was necessary for them to find some one guilty, they did find—at least they said they did—that Mr. Ames had been guilty of bribery, and should therefore be expelled.

The only evidence of bribery before the committee was that of Mr. McComb, which was so sifted as to prove every material statement made by him to be without the shadow of a foundation; but it must have been upon this that the committee based their findings, or else on their own imaginations, for there was nothing else.

As to the influence that was exerted upon these members of Congress who had purchased the stock, the records of Congress show that on the bill instructing the attorney-general to investigate whether the Union Pacific and Central Pacific railroads had not both forfeited their franchises, and directing the withholding of bonds until the matter was decided, each and every one of these members voted for it, with the exception of Mr. Brooks, and he opposed it on special grounds which he then assigned. Mr. Wilson of Iowa was the author of the clause securing the government lien on interest due. Mr. Boutwell forced the collection of the interest, and caused Mr. Ames to fail in business. Mr. Bingham, of Ohio, called up the most stringent bill to protect the interest of the government passed since the legislation of 1864, and advocated it, and it was this that all voted for when the bill overruling Mr. Boutwell's order for collecting the interest came up before the house. Mr. Dawes and Mr. Allison, at the time, were absent at a meeting of conference committees, and so could not vote. The story that Colfax ruled out the resolution of Mr. Washburne, of Wisconsin, fixing freight rates on these roads, is shown by the Congressional Globe to be without foundation. Indeed the committee were justified in finding that these members had not been influenced by reason of the stock they held.

The debate upon these reports lasted two days and evenings and part of the third day, and was participated in by a large number of the members; very few, however, had the courage to stand against the report of the committee. In fact, as the evidence was so bulky, they had not the time to investigate it or study it, and therefore could not discover the fearful errors into which the committee had fallen. In the meantime the Judiciary committee of the House had made a lengthy report, in which they held, adversely to the committee on investigation, that Congress had no right or power to expel a member for acts committed prior to his election as a member of that body.

We shall make no attempt to follow these arguments in this place, many of which were couched in language of purest eloquence and deep research. The one most listened to was that of the most interested party in this unfortunate controversy, that of Oakes Ames, which was read from the clerk's desk. Inasmuch as it presents a most thorough summary of the whole subject-matter, not merely of the evidence elicited, but also the history of the Credit Mobilier and its conection with the Pacific road, we shall ask the privilege of setting it forth entire; and asking for its earnest perusal.

IX.

DEFENCE OF OAKES AMES

AGAINST THE CHARGE OF SELLING TO MEMBERS OF CONGRESS SHARES OF THE CAPITAL STOCK OF THE CREDIT MOBILIER OF AMERICA, WITH INTENT TO BRIBE SAID MEMBERS OF CONGRESS.

Read in the House of Representatives, February 25, 1873.

BEFORE the House proceeds to the consideration of the resolution reported on Tuesday last by the special committee charged with the investigation of alleged transactions with certain members of this body, in the disposition of shares of the capital stock of the Credit Mobilier of America, I desire to submit the following statement:

The charges on which said resolution is based relate to events so intimately connected with a portion of the history of the construction of the Union Pacific railroad that I shall ask the indulgence of the House while I proceed to trace such history in greater detail than would otherwise be necessary.

On the 1st day of July, 1862, was passed and approved an act of Congress, authorizing and providing for the construction of a railroad and telegraph line from the Missouri river to the Pacific ocean. The practicability and importance of such a measure had long been urged by our most sagacious public men, but it failed to receive the sanction of the government, until a great civil war threatened to result in the withdrawal of the States and Territories of the Pacific coast from the authority of the Federal Government. For a variety of reasons, then long before the public, but chiefly to avert the calamity indicated, this act was passed. It was universally esteemed not only a measure of sound policy, but a scheme appealing to the patriotism and loyalty of the capitalists of the United States, as the instrument whereby future separation of the Pacific from the Atlantic States would be rendered forever impossible.

The meeting of commissioners named in the act to carry the same into effect, by the organization of the corporation, was held pursuant to act of Congress, on the first Tuesday of September, 1862. Though composed of a great number of the leading capitalists of the country, and, in addition to the ordinary inducement of pecuniary advantage, acting under the stimulus of patriotic ardor, the meeting failed to accomplish anything beyond the opening of books of subscription. Not a dollar of stock was subscribed or promised, and it was not until about the 27th day of October, 1863—and then only with the explicit understanding on the part of the subscribers that in case of failure to secure future legislation the project must be abandoned—that a' sufficient subscription was obtained to authorize the election of a board of directors. On this subscription was the name of no recognized capitalist. Parties known to the country as wielding large capital in railroad enterprises had studiously avoided all *apparent* association with the enterprise, and in their place appeared a class of comparatively unknown men whose names, when rising to the surface, had been chiefly connected with enterprises involving speculative and extra-hazardous risks. Until the passage of the law heretofore mentioned, nothing was done under this organization beyond such acts as were necessary to preserve the existence of the corporation.

Then came the act of July 2, 1864. Its principal features were as follows: It authorized a reduction of the par value of the shares from one thousand to one hundred dollars, with a corresponding increase in number; it enlarged the land grant from a ten to a twenty-mile limit; it authorized the company to issue first mortgage bonds on its railroad and telegraph, to an amount per mile equal to the amount of United States bonds authorized to be issued to the company in aid of the construction of the road, and made the mortgage securing the same a lien prior to that of the United States; it declared that only one-half of the compensation for services rendered for the government should be required to be applied to the payment of the bonds issued by the government in aid of construction. While thus strengthening the company by these changes, Congress, at the same time, and in the same act, dealt it two well-nigh fatal blows, from the effect of which complete recovery is impossible. It authorized the Kansas Pacific, which was required to effect a junction with the Union Pacific not farther west than the 100th meridian of longitude—a distance of about 247 miles west of the Missouri River—to make such connection at any point westwardly of such initial point deemed practicable or desirable. The result is a rival parallel road connecting with the Union Pacific at a point 516 miles west of the Missouri River—being one-half the length of that road—and claiming equal advantages and facilities in all running connections and interchange of business. It likewise provided that in case the Central Pacific should reach the eastern boundary of California before the Union Pacific should be built to that point, the former company should have the right to extend its road 150 miles eastward, and this power was afterwards enlarged by Congress by act of July 2d, 1866, so as to authorize such extension indefinitely, until the two roads should meet. Thus, by act of Congress, these two corporations were sent forth upon a race across the continent, which finally culminated in the construction of 500 miles of road by each company in a single season, through a desert country, upon a route beset by unparalleled obstacles, and at a necessary cost largely in excess of the most extravagant estimates.

It is in testimony before a committee of the House that, after the impracticability of building the road under the first act had been demonstrated, when it had become apparent that additional aid was necessary to induce capitalists to embark in the enterprise, the late President Lincoln was urgent that Congress should not withhold the additional assistance asked, and that he personally advised the officers of the company to go to Congress for such legislation as would assure the success of the enterprise, declaring it a national necessity, and recommending them to apply for additional concessions, ample to place the construction of the road beyond a peradventure.

Notwithstanding this favorable legislation, no capital was attracted, no additional stock subscribed. On the 8th of August, 1864, a contract for building one hundred miles west from the Missouri river was let to H. M. Hoxie, the only contractor offering to undertake so hazardous a venture. Six months demonstrated his inability to perform his contract, and with the experience of the company in dealing with individual contractors, no course seemed open, except to seek a consolidation of personal means into a corporate body, whereby the pecuniary liability of a large number of persons might be made available to the task of constructing the road, while at the same time enjoying the shelter of corporate liability only. Accordingly, by a contract made March 15, 1865, the Credit Mobilier of America, a corporation created by and organized under the laws of Pennsylvania, in substance assumed the obligations of the Hoxie contract and entered upon its performance. It was soon manifest that even this organization, as then constituted, would be unable to accomplish the work for which it was created. The state of the country and the peculiar local conditions surrounding the enterprise were exceedingly unfavorable to a successful prosecution of the work. Gold was one hundred and fifty; there was no market for the first mortgage bonds, and the government bonds, payable in currency, were of uncertain value and of difficult sale. No eastern railroad connection existed whereby the vast amount of material essential to construction could find reasonable and rapid transportation to the line of the road; it was compelled, instead, to follow the long and tedious route of the Missouri river, at an extraordinary cost for transportation, and without insurance against the perils of the hazardous navigation of that treacherous stream. All materials were high, and all classes of labor scarce, and only to be obtained in limited quantities, at extravagant prices. Add to this the universal distrust in financial circles of the ultimate completion of the road, and the general conviction that when completed it would fail to prove remunerative or profitable, and it is easy to anticipate the result which speedily followed, viz., the practical failure of the new organization to carry forward the work until reinforced by a new class of capitalists, bringing with them larger means and a more powerful influence in the financial world.

Early in September, 1865, it became manifest that the contract could not be performed, and that the work must stop, unless additional strength could be imparted to the corporation. Accordingly, after urgent solicitation and long consideration, myself and others associated with me, for the first time, took an interest in the organization. Its capital stock was increased, additional money was raised, and the work went forward. Under this arrangement two hundred and forty-seven miles of road were built, when, on 16th day of August, 1867, it was superseded by the Oakes Ames contract, so called, and this contract was, on the 15th day of October, 1867, assigned to seven persons, as trustees, and under it six hundred and sixty-seven miles of road were built.

The alleged corrupt transactions imputed to me are all charged to have been initiated in December, 1867. Glance for a moment at the situation of the Union Pacific Company and my connection with it at that time. After a long and nearly ineffectual struggle, the final construction of the road had been assured by my intervention in its affairs. No one doubted that it would be rapidly pushed to completion. Congress had long before, and not at my instance, enacted the laws tendering inducements to the capitalists of the country to embark in the construction of the road, and I and my associates accepted its offers and undertook the work. The company had no reason to apprehend unfriendly or hostile legislation, for every department of the government manifested a friendly attitude, and the whole country was loud in demonstrations of approval of the energy and activity which we had infused into the enterprise. Heads of departments and government officials, of every grade, whose duties brought them in contact with the affairs of the company, were clamorous for increased speed of construction, and never lost an opportunity of expressing approval of the work and urging it forward. It had never entered my mind that the company would ask for or need additional legislation, and it would have been difficult to find a man so reckless of popular opinion as to have lent himself to a crusade against an organization whose praises everywhere filled the press and were on the lips of the people. As a matter of history, no legislation, at all effecting the pecuniary interests of the company, was asked for for three years and a half after the date of the alleged sales by me of Credit Mobilier stock, and then only in settlement of a purely judicial question, suddenly and without warning sprung upon it, in a critical period of its fortunes, and in relation to which no controversy had ever before been made. Under no other state of affairs, and in no other attitude of the government, could I for a moment have been induced to assume the enormous responsibility entailed by a contract involving a liability of forty-seven millions of dollars. To undertake the construction of a railroad, at any price, for a distance of nearly seven hundred miles, in a desert and unexplored country, its line crossing three mountain ranges, at the highest elevations yet attempted on this continent, extending through a country swarming with hostile Indians, by whom locating engineers and conductors of construction trains were repeatedly killed and scalped at their work, upon a route destitute of water, except as supplied by water trains hauled from one to one hundred and fifty miles, to thousands of men and animals engaged in construction, the immense mass of material, iron, ties, lumber, timber, provisions, and supplies necessary, to be transported from five hundred to fifteen hundred miles, I admit might well, in the light of subsequent history and the mutations of opinion, be regarded as the freak of a madman, if it did not challenge the recognition of a higher motive, namely, the desire to connect my name conspicuously with the greatest public work of the present century. It is by no means strange that my credit with conservative financiers like Governor Washburn should have been shaken, and that he should have hastened to call in loans which, in his judgment, this contract proved to be in unsafe hands.

Under these circumstances, with all legislation sought granted, and no future action of Congress to be asked for or feared, it is charged that I "have been guilty of selling to members of Congress shares of stock in the Credit Mobilier of America, for prices below the true value of such stock, with intent to influence the votes and decisions of such members in matters to be brought before Congress for action."

If this charge is true, it is predicated upon three facts, all of which should be shown to the satisfaction of this body, in order to justify the extreme measures recommended by the committee.

First. The shares must have been sold at prices so manifestly and palpably below the true value as to conclusively presume the expectation of some other pecuniary advantage in addition to the price paid.

Second. The shares must have been of such a nature as that their ownership would create in the holder a corrupt purpose to shape legislation in the interest of the seller.

Third. Some distinct and specific matter or thing to be brought before Congress, and on which the votes and decisions of members are sought to be influenced, should be alleged and proved.

It is by no means clear, from the testimony, that the stock was sold at a price less than its true value. It was not on the market; it had no market value. Unlike an ordinary marketable commodity, it had no current price, and the amount for which it could be sold depended upon the temperament of the buyer, and his inclination to assume extraordinary risks on the one hand, or his tendency to conservative and strictly solid investments on the other. It is in proof before a committee of this House, by witnesses largely interested in railroad construction and operation, and of great financial ability and strength, that when this stock was offered to them at par, it was instantly declined, by reason of the enormous risks involved in the enterprises on which its value depended. These capitalists believed that all the capital invested in the stock was jeopardized, and the venture was declined on the rule that no promise of profit justifies a prudent man in embarking in any enterprise in which all the capital invested is liable to be sunk. Apart from some proof that a small amount of this stock changed hands between persons addicted to speculation, at about one hundred and fifty, nothing is shown in reference to its value, except that it was not on the market, and had no ascertained price. To overturn the presumption of innocence and substitute the conclusive imputation of guilt, from the simple fact of such a transaction occurring between men who had long maintained the most friendly personal relations, — of whom nothing was asked, and by whom nothing was promised, — is to overturn all the safeguards afforded persons and property by the common law, and in lieu thereof establish an inquisitorial code, under which no man's reputation is safe.

It has been assumed that the ownership of Credit Mobilier stock necessarily created in the holder a personal and pecuniary interest in procuring Congressional legislation favorable to the Union Pacific Railroad company, or preventing legislation adverse to it. At the date of the alleged distribution of Credit Mobilier stock, the Oakes Ames contract had been made, and was in progress of execution. It was completed, and the road covered by the contract turned over to the company about the close of the year 1868. Not until two years after was any legislation asked for by the company, and then it was such as arose out of exigencies presented by the action of the government in reversing a long-continued and uniform previous policy, which could not, by any possibility, have been foreseen or anticipated. The stock depended for its value upon the connection of the Credit Mobilier with the Oakes Ames contract, which was simply in the capacity of a guarantor of its execution, whereby a certain class of its stockholders became entitled to participate in the profits of that contract in money. There is no provision of the Oakes Ames contract, the assignment thereof, or of the triplicate agreement, whereby a stockholder became entitled to any of the securities of the Union Pacific Railroad Company, or in any way interested in their value. The profits derived, if any, were to be, and were, in cash. When the Oakes Ames contract was completed, and the consideration thereof divided in cash to the several parties entitled, in due proportion, the interest of a holder of Credit Mobilier stock in the Union Pacific Railroad Company, and every thing pertaining to it, was at an end. In other words, the stipulations of that contract, and the cash profits derivable therefrom, were the end and the beginning, — the centre and circumference, — the absolute measure of the pecuniary interest of a holder of Credit Mobilier stock in 1868. To say that the Washburne bill, which professed to deal exclusively with the operation of the road, in the hands of the company, after it had been built and turned over by the contractors, was a measure feared, and to protect the railroad company, against which the stock in question was sold to members of Congress, seems to me to invoke the last extreme of credulity.

It is impossible to impute to me the purpose to corruptly influence members of Congress, by conferring upon them pecuniary benefit without adequate consideration, unless the benefit conferred is of such a character as to necessarily create an inclination to aid the donor to the detriment of the public. There is but one escape from this position, and that leads to a lower deep. It may be said that the giving by any person, and the receiving by a member of Congress of any gratuity whatever, or, what is identical therewith, selling and buying at an inadequate price, imports corruption in both the giver and receiver, the buyer and seller. Whoever proclaims this doctrine should instantly set on foot the inquiry how many railroad presidents and superintendents have presented to members of Congress the value of transportation over their respective railroad lines, and by whom the same has been received, to the end that justice may be done, and the one presented for indictment, and the other for expulsion. The dimensions and value of the gratuity have nothing to do with the question. There is no middle ground on which to stand.

For the first time in the history of any tribunal, this body has before it an alleged offender without an offense. Any person accused in the courts of the country, under like circumstances, might well, when called upon to plead to the indictment, insist that it failed to charge a crime. I am charged by the committee with the purpose of corrupting certain members of Congress, while it, at the same time, declares said members to have been unconscious of my purpose, and fails to indicate the subject of the corruption. In other words, the purpose to corrupt is inferred, where the effect of corrupting could not by possibility be produced, and where no subject for corruption existed. No lawyer who values his reputation will assert that an indictment for bribery could stand for an instant in a common-law court, without specifically alleging who was the briber, who was bribed, and what precise measure, matter, or thing was the subject of bribery. There can be no attempt to bribe without the hope and purpose of corruptly influencing some person or persons in respect to some particular act. Until, therefore, it is alleged and shown not only who tendered a bribe, but who accepted or refused it, and what was the specific subject-matter of the bribery, any conviction which may follow the alleged offense must rest upon the shifting and unstable foundation of individual caprice, and not upon the solid rock of justice administered under the restraints of law.

I shall not enter upon a discussion of the jurisdiction of this body over offenses alleged to have been committed during a previous Congress, leaving that question for such additional comment as the lawyers of the House choose to make. The position, however, that the fault — if such exists — is a continuing offense, is so extraordinary, and fruitful of such fatal consequences, that I cannot forbear a reference to it. Since the Credit Mobilier stock sold by me passed into the hands of the several members of Congress referred to in the report, I have been, in the judgment of the committee, a perpetual and chronic offender against the dignity and honor of the House, and, so far as my own volition is concerned, must so continue to the end of the world. So long as a single share of this stock shall not be restored, but shall remain in the hands of the several receivers, or either or any of them, my offense goes on, and I am bereft of the power to stop it. And yet, notwithstanding the world is now apprised of my alleged corrupt intentions — and no member of Congress can be ignorant of them — the parties who alone have the power, but fail to release me from the necessity of continuing my offenses by return of the stock, are themselves without blame, and in no way obnoxious to the sins laid upon me. The committee declare that want of knowledge alone of the corrupt intention of the seller excused the buyer, while holding and owning the proceeds of the sale. Now that such knowledge is everywhere and among all men, how can this, in the absence of a restoration of the stock or its proceeds, be a living, continuing, perpetual crime in the seller and not in the buyer?

I beg to be correctly understood. I allege nothing against those members of the House who purchased Credit Mobilier stock. I am simply following the reasoning of the committee to its logical results. I make no assault upon any man or class of men; but I earnestly protest against being chosen the victim of a line of reasoning and assertion, in my judgment unjust, partial, unsound, inconsistent, and inconclusive,—calculated, if endorsed, to bring this body into disrepute, and repugnant to the sense of justice and fair play embedded in the hearts of the American people.

Reference is made by the committee to the act of February 26, 1863, and, after setting out the same, the following language is used:—" In the judgment of the committee, the facts reported in regard to Mr. Ames and Mr. Brooks would have justified their conviction under the above-recited statute, and subjected them to the penalties therein provided." I beg gentlemen to note the entire section carefully and critically, and verify the assertion I now make that every penalty denounced upon him who shall " promise, offer, or give, or cause, or procure to be promised, offered, or given," * * * " any valuable thing" * * * " to any member of Congress " * * * " with intent to influence his vote on any matter pending or to be brought before him," is alike launched with impartial severity against any member, officer, or person who shall in anywise accept or receive the same, NOT *knowingly, wilfully*, or *feloniously* receive the same, but IN ANYWISE accept or receive the same. Mark the language: " And the member, officer, or person who shall IN ANYWISE accept or receive the same, or any part thereof, shall be liable to an indictment as for a high crime and misdemeanor, and shall, upon conviction thereof, be fined not exceeding ten times the amount so offered, promised, or given, and imprisoned in a penetentiary not exceeding ten years."

Again I protest against the conclusion of the committee, which makes this unequal, partial, and discriminating allotment of the penalties of a statute designed by its framers impartially to strike or shelter all to whom it applies. Whatever result may be reached here, none can doubt that in the courts of the country there will be one law for all.

Aside, then, from the letters addressed to Mr. McComb, it is impossible to infer the motives attributed to me by the committee. Mr. McComb claimed that about $20,000 of the $25,000 of stock voted me to fulfil my obligations to my friends, should be given to him for distribution to his friends, and the letters to him were written to show that I was selling the stock in small quantities to my friends, and could not give his friends the entire amount they desired. A perfect understanding of the circumstances under which these letters were written, and a candid consideration of their object and purpose, must, I think, carry to any unbiased mind the conviction that my motives were very far from those ascribed to me. Dr. Durant, Mr. McComb, and myself, were each anxious to secure as large a portion as possible of the shares of Credit Mobilier stock, and professedly for the same purpose; namely, for disposition to those persons with whom, from past favors or personal friendship, we were willing to share opportunities of profitable investment. I had no desire or expectation to further enrich myself, for my sole object was to get and retain as much of this stock as possible, to be used in redeeming obligations of the character named. These obligations had been incurred not only to members of Congress, but to many private citizens in no way connected with official life; they had been contracted early in the year 1867, when the stock could not be sold above par, and it was to meet these contracts that I made special efforts to obtain the stock. In doing so, I took it, not for my individual use, but as trustee, for the sole purpose of conveying it to the parties entitled, and it would have been a breach of faith in me to have asked or taken a price in excess of the par value, notwithstanding it may have in the meantime advanced. No distinction was made between members of Congress and unofficial friends, and in performing the obligations I had incurred, I sold to both alike stock at its par value, in accordance with my agreement. When, therefore, Mr. McComb objected to my receiving so large an amount, and entered upon a struggle to prevent it, I naturally addressed to him such arguments and considerations as, in my judgment, would make the deepest impression upon his mind. It so happened that, in the prosperity and success of the Union Pacific Railroad Company, Mr. McComb and myself had a common and identical interest; and I therefore urged upon him that I had so disposed of the stock as to enhance the general strength and influence of the company, for whose welfare his solicitude was not less than my own. It is no sufficient answer to this to say that the statement contained in the letters on which I most relied to influence his mind, I now concede contained expressions liable to be construed against the purity of my motives. Tried by the test of casual and confidential letters, often written hastily, and under circumstances and surroundings entirely different from those in the light of which they are interpreted—framed for a specific purpose, and to accomplish a particular end—their collateral and incidental bearings not reflected upon and deliberately weighed, but flung off hastily in the instant press of business, and the freedom of that personal confidence ordinarily existing between parties jointly concerned in financial schemes or enterprises of public improvement, he would indeed be a cautious, a prudent, a wise, and almost perfect man, who could emerge from such an ordeal completely free from the suspicion of fault.

I wish, therefore, to declare, in the broadest sense of which language is capable, that in writing the McComb letters, I had alone in view the objects above enumerated; that I never for an instant imagined that from them could be extracted proof of the motive and purpose of corrupting members of Congress—motives and purposes which I solemnly declare I never entertained. The insignificant amounts of stock sold to each member with whom I had dealings; the proven fact that I never urged its purchase, and the entire lack of secrecy—ordinarily the badge of evil purposes—in these transactions, ought, in my judgment, to stand as a conclusive refutation of the offences charged. And above and beyond this, I submit that a long and busy life spent in the prosecution of business pursuits, honorable to myself and useful to mankind, and a reputation hitherto without stain, should of its weight overcome and outweigh charges solely upheld by the unconsidered and unguarded utterances of confidential business communications.

A vast amount of error has been disseminated and prejudice aroused in the minds of many by incorrect and extravagant statements of the profits accruing from the different contracts for the construction of the road, and especially that commonly known as the Oakes Ames contract. The risk, the state of the country, thé natural obstacles, the inflation of the currency and consequent exorbitant prices of labor and material, the Indian perils, the unparalleled speed of construction, and the clamorous demands of the country for speedy completion, seem to be forgotten, and the parties connected with the Credit Mobilier and the construction of the road are now to be tried by a standard foreign to the time and circumstances under which the work was done. It is said that when the failure to secure the necessary amount of cash subscriptions to the stock was proved, and it became manifest that the only medium through which the work could go on was by a constructing company, which would undertake to build the road and take the securities and stock of the company in payment—when the whole enterprise had come to a complete halt, and was set in motion by my individual credit and means, and that of my associates—the enterprise should have been abandoned.

Were it possible to present that question to the same public sentiment, the same state of national opinion, which existed at the time the exigency arose, I would willingly and gladly go to Congress and the country on that issue. But I am denied that justice, and the motives and transactions of one period are to be judged by the prejudices of another, at an hour when the fluctuations of opinion are extreme and violent, beyond the experience of former times. The actual cost, in money, of building the road was about seventy millions of dollars, and all statements of a less cost are based upon mere estimates of engineers who never saw the work, and utterly fail to grasp the conditions under which it was prosecuted. The actual profit on this expenditure, estimating the securities and stock at their market value when received in payment, was less than ten millions of dollars, as can be demonstrably established in any court. It is in testimony before a committee of the House, by witnesses who have spent their lives as contractors, as well as those who have been builders, owners, and operators of some of the great trunk lines of the country, that for twenty years past the ordinary method of building railroads has been through the medium of constructing companies; that few, if any, roads involving a large outlay of capital are built in any other way; that a profit of from twenty to thirty per cent. is not unreasonable in any case, and that upon the construction of the Union Pacific railroad, estimating it with reference to the magnitude of the work and the risk incurred, no man could reasonably object to a profit of fifty per cent. The like evidence is given by a government director, long intimately acquainted with the manifold difficulties and embarrassments encountered, and who has not yet outlived the recollection and realization of them.

So far as I am pecuniarily concerned, it would have been better that I had never heard of the Union Pacific railroad. At its completion the company found itself in debt about six millions of dollars, the burden of which fell upon individuals, myself among others. The assumption of the large portion of this liability allotted to me, followed by others necessary to keep the road in operation until there should be developed in the inhospitable region through which it runs a business affording revenue sufficient to meet running expenses and interest, finally culminated in events familiar to the public, whereby losses were incurred greatly in excess of all profit derived by me from the construction of the road.

What then has the government received as the fruits of the connection of the Credit Mobilier with the Union Pacific Railroad Company, and the transactions now, under consideration? By the terms of its charter it agreed, among other things, to loan the company for thirty years its bonds to certain amounts per mile, and until their maturity one-half the earnings on account of government transportation should be retained, to be applied in repayment to the government of whatever interest might in the meantime be paid on the bonds by the United States.

The company in turn, by acceptance of the charter, agreed to pay the United States the amount due on the bonds at their maturity, and to perform certain services. Without asking additional legislation, or being called upon to resist obnoxious legislation, except wherein this contract had been disregarded and ignored by the government, the road has been completed and successfully operated throughout its entire line now nearly four years.

No complaint has ever come up from any quarter of any failure to faithfully perform its obligations to the government, both in respect to transportation services and its pecuniary obligations. In the only instance in which it has differed from any department of the government, the variance has been upon a purely judicial question, upon which the courts have been open to the United States, but closed to us. The government made itself the creditor of the Union Pacific Company, tying its debtor hand and foot with a multiplicity of stipulations, and then refused to submit their interpretation to its own courts. That it has so far reaped the principal benefit of the bargain cannot be denied. Official statements of the postmaster-general are before the House, which show that for the six years ending June 30, 1872, the saving to the government upon the transportation of postal matter alone by reason of the construction of the Union Pacific railroad, assuming the amount carried to be equal to that transported previous to its construction, has been $643,579.55. But the amount of postal matter has been over six times greater by rail than by stage, so that the real saving is not less than $3,861,477.30. Even this result fails to represent the increased speed of carriage and convenience of handling and distribution afforded by postal cars to the employees of the department accompanying the mails, thus insuring safety and regularity in delivery. A like statement from the war department shows the saving upon military transportation for the same time to have been $6,507,282.85. No official estimates are before the House for the saving upon transportation of Indian goods, for the navy department, or of coin or currency, but they may be safely aggregated at not less than $2,500,000. This gives a total saving for the six years ending June 30, 1872, of the sum of $12,868,760.15. The Secretary of the Treasury in a communication to the House, bearing date May 20, 1872, in answer to a resolution calling for such information, estimates the amount of interest and principal which will be due from the Union Pacific Railroad Company, at the maturity of the government bonds, at the present rate of payment, at $58,156,746.98. Assuming that the saving to the government of all the different classes of transportation in the future will be the same as in the past (a supposition entirely on the side of the United States, for it will in fact increase in almost geometrical progression), and the result is a total saving, at the date of the maturity of the bonds of $64,343,880.75, a sum in excess of the principal and interest due at that time to the amount of $6,187,053.77. In other words, if at the maturity of the bonds not one cent of interest or principal was paid, but on the other hand was entirely lost, the government would be the gainer in money to the amount of $6,187,053.77.

All this is solid gain, involving no consequential element, and susceptible of exact computation. To attempt to grasp the national benefits which lie outside the domain of figures, but are embodied in the increased prosperity, wealth, population, and power of the nation, overtasks the most vivid imagination. When the rails were joined on Promontory Summit, May 10, 1869, the Pacific and the Atlantic, Europe and Asia, the East and the West, pledged themselves to that perpetual amity out of which should spring an interchange of the most precious and costly commodities known to traffic, thus assuring a commerce whose tide should ebb to and fro across the continent by this route for ages to come. Utah was then an isolated community, with no industry but agriculture, and those manufactures necessary to a poor and frugal people. In 1872 it shipped ten millions of silver to the money centres of the world, and is now demonstrated to be the richest mineral storehouse on the continent. An institution repugnant to the moral sense of the Christian world is fast yielding to the civilizing contact of the outer travel made possible by the construction of the railway. Many believe it has already substantially solved the perplexing problem of polygamy. A vast foreign immigration, bringing with it from Europe an immense aggregate sum of money, has already been distributed far out on the line of the road, and its means and muscle are fast subjecting the lately sparsely-peopled territories of Colorado, Wyoming, Montana, and Idaho to the uses of an enterprising and rapidly-increasing population. A steady and copious flow of British capital is pouring into the mines of Colorado and Utah. The Indians have been pacified; fruitless and costly hostile military expeditions, frequent elsewhere, have ceased in the vicinity of its line, and the facility and speed of communication afforded by the railroad enables the government to offer adequate protection to the frontier with a handful of troops, and at the same time dispense with large garrisons and fortified posts, hitherto maintained at fabulous cost. The countless herds of Texas are moving up to occupy the grazing grounds of the buffalo in the valleys and canons shadowed by the Rocky Mountains. A region of boundless natural resources, lately unknown, unexplored, and uninhabited, dominated by savages, has been reclaimed, hundreds of millions added to the wealth of the nation, and the bonds of fraternal and commercial union between the East and West strengthened beyond the power of civil discord to sever.

Does any one—yearning with solicitude lest the United States, which has made this fortunate bargain, should fail to receive each cent due at the precise moment it may be demanded by its officers— doubt the ability of the company to perform its obligations and pay the last dollar due, long before the maturity of the bonds? Four years ago the road was opened, without local business, with no considerable through traffic, and in the dawn of the friendly relations between the United States and those Asiatic nations which now bid fair to prove the source of its largest and most lucrative business. The conservative capitalists of the country believed it would bankrupt any organization which undertook to operate it. Four years have reversed that opinion, and now the same men are putting forth their best efforts to secure the benefit of a close traffic-connection, and perhaps ultimate ownership. Twenty-four years ago there was scarcely a mile of railroad west of Lake Erie, and no connecting line west of Buffalo. Let him who would rightly estimate the future of this company go back to the year 1848, and thence forward to the present time, trace the growth and development of that portion of the United States lying west of the great lakes, and he will be able to approximate the coming history of the region through which this road stretches for a thousand miles, and of the trade and products and commodities of which it is to be the great commercial artery. There is but one power that can destroy its ability to perform all its obligations to the government; there is but one agency that can render it incapable of paying all its indebtedness, to the last dollar, namely, the Congress of the United States. It alone can so cripple, weaken, or destroy the company as to make the loan of the government to it a *total loss*.

These, then, are my offences: that I have risked reputation, fortune, everything, in an enterprise of incalculable benefit to the government, from which the capital of the world shrank; that I have sought to strengthen the work, thus rashly undertaken, by invoking the charitable judgment of the public upon its obstacles and embarrassments; that I have had friends, some of them in official life, with whom I have been willing to share advantageous opportunities of investment; that I have kept to the truth through good and evil report, denying nothing, concealing nothing, reserving nothing. Who will say that I alone am to be offered up a sacrifice to appease a public clamor or expiate the sins of others? Not until such an offering is made will I believe it possible. But if this body shall so order that it can best be purified by the choice of a single victim, I shall accept its mandate, appealing with unfaltering confidence to the impartial verdict of history for that vindication which it is proposed to deny me here.

X.

THE VOTE OF CENSURE.

IN consequence of the report of the Judiciary committee already alluded to, and a feeling on the part of many members that the evidence would not warrant the conviction, it was growing apparent that the report of the committee would not be sustained, and that the expulsion of these members would not follow. Mr. Sargent, of California, moved to substitute for the resolutions offered by the committee, the following:—

Whereas, by the report of the special committee herein, it appears that the acts charged against members of this House in connection with the Credit Mobilier of America, occurred more than five years ago, and long before the election of such persons to this Congress, two elections by the people having intervened; and, whereas grave doubts exist as to the rightful exercise by this House of its power to expel a member for offenses committed by such member long before his election thereto, and not connected with such election: therefore,

Resolved, That the special committee be discharged from the further consideration of this subject.

Resolved, That the House absolutely condemns the conduct of OAKES AMES, a member of this House from

Massachusetts, in seeking to procure Congressional attention to the affairs of a corporation in which he was interested, and whose interest directly depended upon the legislation of Congress, by inducing members of Congress to invest in the stocks of said corporation.

Resolved, That this House absolutely condemns the conduct of JAMES BROOKS, a member of this House from New York, for the use of his position as government director of the Union Pacific Railroad, and a member of this House, to procure the assignment to himself or family, of stock in the Credit Mobilier of America, a corporation having a contract with the Union Pacific railroad, and whose interests depended directly upon the legislation of Congress.

On this motion to substitute, the yeas and nays were called, and with the following result. Yeas, 115; nays, 110; not voting, 15. So it was agreed to substitute these resolutions for those offered by the committee.

The question then came upon the resolution condemning the action of Oakes Ames, and it was agreed to by a vote of 182 yeas, 36 nays, 22 not voting.

Upon the resolution condemning the action of James Brooks, the vote stood: 174 yeas, 32 nays, 34 not voting.

And so the resolutions were each agreed to.

During these proceedings Mr. Ames occupied a seat on the floor of the House, immediately in front of the Speaker, in plain view of all. He realized the situation in which he was placed, and felt deeply, keenly, the disgrace that was being placed upon him. He sat there silent, immovable, a deathly pallor on his countenance, calmly waiting for the awful decision. Mr. Brooks occupied his own seat, looking more like a corpse than a human being. Those were awful moments to these men, as name after name was called and recorded on the everlasting pages of history, where generations yet unborn might come, and, reading, point the finger of scorn at those names thus shrouded in eternal infamy. A whole life was centered in those few moments. All hope was lost, all honor gone. When the decision had been announced and the awful sentence recorded, there "ensued upon the floor of Congress a scene without parallel. Men who had just joined in the vote of condemnation against Mr. Ames, gathered around him to ask his pardon for having done so. They said to him, 'we know that you are innocent; but we had to do it in order to satisfy our constituents.'"

This scene is a fact, and the names of those who thus spoke can be given. What virtuous men to sit in judgment upon their fellow-men! How noble the hearts that could thus consign to infamy a fellow being! Years after, others have confessed their vote was given as it was solely on account of personal hopes. It presents a picture of depravity by the side of which all the acts *charged* against Oakes Ames stand out as honorable in the extreme.

Congress soon adjourned, and the terms of service of Oakes Ames and James Brooks were at an end. They returned to their respective homes only to die.

In a few weeks they were no more. The people of the whole nation soon began to realize that in the death of Mr. Ames the country had lost a great benefactor — a man through whose instrumentality the greatest achievement of the present age had been successfully completed. There is no doubt but the disgrace thus placed upon him ended his life. Whatever opinion the world at large may have entertained of the man, however deep was the feeling against him in general, those who knew him, and who had been associated with him, could not be made to believe that dishonor or guilt had ever lurked within his heart. In all his private relations his name was pure and spotless. In his business his honor and integrity were proverbial. Still he may not have been a man who would impress those who knew him not, with a sense of his greatness. That was reserved for those who could become intimate with him, and understand him. He was not given to niceties, or to small matters. He might not be able to discern fine-drawn distinctions, but his mind was comprehensive enough to grasp the most gigantic schemes, and understand them. To him the success of the Pacific road was beyond doubting. He believed it, and he was willing to risk his entire fortune — as, in fact, he did — in its construction. He beheld the vast benefit it would be to the country, and he saw the stream of commerce that was to roll on forever over its line. He saw the unity it would establish between all sections of the country, and comprehended the patriotic influence it would ever exert. He became interested in the Pacific road at a critical hour of its fortunes, and he gave it his means, his energy, his life.

While we cannot say that he was insensible to gain, still those who knew him best can never be made to doubt that there was a large element of patriotism in the views which induced him to take the position he did in constructing this great highway from the river, through the wilderness, and over the mountains to the ocean. His work was finished in the same spirit in which he worked all through his connection with it; and at the time when he ought to have received his reward, when he should have been entitled to a life of honor and ease, he found himself assailed in the most most wanton manner, and his name and fame forever tarnished.

When he returned from Washington, at the close of his Congressional labors, he was met by the citizens of his home with a demonstration which showed their absolute confidence in his honor, and they gave expression of their love for him in a manner that was most impressive. Two months later they followed him to his grave and wept over his remains.

The flight of time has not failed to bring back to the memory of Oakes Ames the vindication that was denied him on the floor of Congress. Every position which he took regarding the Credit Mobilier or the Union Pacific road has been sustained whenever brought before our tribunals of justice. The anticipations and predictions of the future of that road have been fulfilled. It has proven a success in every way, and the country through which it was built has been developed beyond the wildest prophecies.

The stockholders of the Union Pacific road have lately erected a monument to the memory of Oakes and Oliver Ames, on the highest ground between the Atlantic and Pacific slopes crossed by the road. While the road itself is the grandest monument that could be erected to the memory of any man, it is but appropriate that this outward sign should be made as a further evidence of the appreciation of their business enterprise and sagacity, and their great merit. There may it ever stand, overlooking the work they carried through; and those who journey over the road cannot avoid the feeling that this is but a just recognition for their services; and when the whole of this great struggle shall have become fully known, no doubt can longer exist as to the loyalty of their motives and actions.

XI.

THE CREDIT MOBILIER OF TO-DAY.

FROM this time forward the Credit Mobilier has lived only in history. The work which it was commissioned to do had been completed — at the date of this vote of censure, three years — and since then has never been heard of, save as spoken of in connection with this last disgraceful scene in its history. Why did it assume so great importance? What were the causes which brought it forth so prominently? These causes have already been alluded to, viz., the political influence that could be created by and through it. Undoubtedly had its purposes, its objects, its work been understood and appreciated, it would never have been heard of after its work was finished. There is an element in the politics of all countries which will grasp every incident that will tend to inflame with prejudice the minds of the people against any party or any individual. Party success overcomes and controls the judgment of party advocates, and those events which in themselves may be pure and innocent, are distorted and made to appear impure and corrupt. Our own country is certainly no exception to this spirit. Our party leaders are not opponents to the rule that success will justify any means used to attain it. Party feeling runs high in our land, and the advantages offered to party leaders to prejudice public opinion are singularly attractive, for in the hands of the people lie all power, and upon them rests the entire responsibility of good government. The jealous care with which our liberties have been governed, the deep love that has been instilled within our hearts for our institutions, and the patriotic desire of every American to see those liberties sustained, those institutions perpetuated, oftentimes make us forget to examine into the merits of the arguments presented, and we condemn where we should praise, and praise where we should condemn. We do not stop to consider consequences, but too oft imbibe within us the very feelings of prejudice which are thrown in our way. We see an action which appears to be born of corruption, or to hold within its hands elements of evil, and straightway we condemn, never stopping to look at its real work or object, never considering whether or not that very appearance is not artificial, and has been pictured to us, by skilful partisans, for no other purpose than their own benefit and advantage. No cry in all our country has so powerful an effect or exerts so great an influence upon public opinion as that which tells us our liberties are in danger of being destroyed by corruption in places of high trust and honor in our national councils. So it was when, in the excitement of a presidential campaign, the cry of Credit Mobilier was raised, — when the declaration was made that corruption the most flagrant had been unearthed among the members of Congress,—when the names of representatives and senators, and other high officials, were given to the country as those who had enriched themselves from the public treasury and had used their positions and their honor for their own gain; it was not strange that the whole country should be aroused, and that society should be stirred to its very foundation. The proof presented was so direct and strong that those whose names were thus paraded before the country dared not face the storm of indignation, and knew not how to explain their positions. In their dilemma they took that course which seemed to afford the easiest and surest escape, and denied all connection.

Where was the wrong? where was the guilt? The people could not understand; the politicians themselves did not comprehend the relation of the Credit Mobilier, or if comprehending they felt unable to state the case so that the people should be able to understand. In the excitement that prevailed matters became so complicated that when the investigation ended, when all the evidence had been collected, every one seemed more in doubt than ever. The public had become more and more convinced that the government had been defrauded, and all parties and classes united in the cry for the punishment of the guilty. The committees of investigation, in view of all this cry of alarm, became so biased that they were impressed in the same manner, and their reports were written more to appease the public, and insure their own safety and continuance in power, than to arrive at exact justice. The recommendations of the Polland committee were shown and proven to be without any authority, and that expulsion, under the circumstances, would be against every law and precedent in parliamentary history. It would have been the establishment of a precedent so wrong and unjust that there would be danger of its overturning the very foundations of the liberty they pretended to be anxious to save. So clear, so plain were the objections to those recommendations set forth, that even their most hotheaded advocate held back in fear, and as a last and final resort the vote of censure was substituted and passed. But it was not passed because it was just and merited, not because those who voted upon it believed it was right, but because the cry throughout the country was for some sort of condemnation, and those men dared not face their constituents with any other record of their votes. No doubt there were many honest, honorable men in that body who voted according to their convictions, who believed that censure to be just, and thought in voting it that they were doing themselves credit and freeing their country from the great stain of disgrace that was upon it. Yet those men could not have had an opportunity to investigate this subject, did not understand it, and from the reports of the committee became more and more uncertain regarding it; and so, taking the reasoning of the committee in all their false positions as correct, voted as they did.

The Wilson committee failed utterly and completely to understand the relations between the Credit Mobilier and the Union Pacific road, and between that road and the government. Their conclusions have been shown, in the highest court of justice in our land, to be founded in error, and to be absolutely wrong. The Supreme Court of the United States has decided that the government was not wronged; that every obligation imposed upon the road has been faithfully performed; that neither the Credit Mobilier nor the trustees, who held the contracts for building the road, had wronged any one, unless it might be some *bona-fide* stockholder of the road, who took no part in its construction, and there was no proof or evidence of such holders. Common sense would teach us that the government was not wronged, when we consider the nature of its claim upon the road. Its credit alone was loaned; it took a security of its own choosing; and though those contractors had incurred an expense of $500,000 per mile in the construction of the road it would not have affected the security of the government. That security was a second mortgage, subject only to a first mortgage of the same amount. If the road had been built for only $50,000,000 — the lowest estimate that could be given under the most favorable circumstances, and the amount which the Wilson committee erroneously claim as its actual cost — still the government's security would have been precisely the same, a second mortgage of the same amount that it now is, subject to a first mortgage of the same amount. Whatever was more than this, whatever further obligations were incurred, became subordinate to the claim of the government, and so no wrong could be done in that way. The prejudice of the past has cleared away to such an extent that the people can be brought to understand this; and when they see that every position taken by the managers of the Credit Mobilier has been upheld in our highest courts of justice; when they have seen that every prediction of the Ameses regarding the prosperity of the road has been more than fulfilled; when they see that the loan of the government will be paid at its maturity by the very means provided in the beginning; when they see the extraordinary advantages that have come to the whole country through the building of that road; when they see the vast volume of commerce that rolls along from the Atlantic to the Pacific, then they become willing to listen to the voice of reason, and cast aside their prejudices, in an attempt to understand and appreciate all that has been done.

When, also, they come to view, with impartial eyes, the connection of members of Congress with the Credit Mobilier; when they comprehend the circumstances under which that stock was held; when they ascertain that there was not then, nor for years after, any legislation before Congress affecting the Pacific roads, that no further legislation was desired, asked for, or feared; when they consider that the contract, under which profits were to come, if come at all, had been made, and was being executed, and that the government had not the right to violate a contract legally made, as the courts have decided this was; when they read the conclusions of the very committee who charge bribery that no one had been bribed, that no member had been influenced in his actions by holding the stock, and that the holding of the stock would not even have a tendency to create an interest that would influence the action of a member of Congress; and when they reflect upon the extreme littleness of the reputed bribe, and its insignificance in comparison with the risk of exposure, how can any other conclusion be reached than that no bribe was offered, no bribe accepted, and no bribery thought of; that members of Congress not only held the stock, but held it rightfully, and with no corrupting influence connected therewith.

Then, again, when looking at all this, when understanding that the government was not, could not, be wronged by the action of the Credit Mobilier; when they understand that the connection of members of Congress with the stock was honorable and right, and that no bribery was attempted, or thought of; when they remember that the sole charge of bribery came from a witness whose testimony was shown, by the most conclusive evidence, to be perjury in every material point, how can any other conclusion be held than that Oakes Ames, in all his acts, was a conscientious and an honest man, and that the vote of censure passed upon him was the most unjust and shameful event in the whole history of Congress.

How all this might have been avoided had men been truthful! No stain rests upon those who came forward and acknowledged their owning the stock. The names of Dawes, and Henry Wilson, and Logan, and Bingham, and John F. Wilson, and others like them, are pure and unspotted, and no thought is ever given them in that respect. The people still honor them; those living are entrusted with high office; those dead have their memory enshrined in the hearts of the people. To Brooks, and Patterson, and Colfax, the finger of scorn is ever held, because they denied the truth, and their word was proven false. They have sunk into a political grave, never again to be trusted with places of honor, or to have their memories, when dead, consecrated in the hearts of their countrymen. In this same list would be classed the name of Garfield, had he not, after he had been cowardly enough to falsify his word, and attempt to blacken the name of his associate and friend, and after he found his word was proven false, by evidence too strong to be overcome, had the wisdom to hold his tongue, and let the whole matter rest in quietness, feeling sure that if no further notice was taken of it, time would lead to its being forgotten.

The Credit Mobilier is still an organization. Its charter is still in force, but its power is gone. Its stock is being gradually absorbed into one common vortex, so that now only about one-fourth is outstanding. There are some questions yet remaining as to its assets, and claims have been made against the Union Pacific Railroad, and a suit is now pending in the courts in Boston for the recovery of $2,000,000, which the Credit Mobilier claims is due from the road. No decision has been reached, and nothing can be said as to the result. Should this claim be sustained, the stock of the Credit Mobilier will be of value; but, as is more than probable, if this suit should be decided adverse to the Credit Mobilier, its stock will be of no value whatever. Its existence thus lies upon the uncertain decision of a suit, and it is more than likely ere another year shall pass, the Credit Mobilier will be among the organizations of the past. Its history may be a pleasant and interesting one in many respects, and in others the extreme opposite. With its life were linked the fortunes of many. Perhaps never in any organization of equal capital has there ever been associated so much wealth, energy, and ability as in this. Its managers were at all times men of the most extraordinary talents, and whose names have almost been household words throughout the land. Its achievements have been the most wonderful ever seen in this country, and the results that have been reached through its work, have done more to build up the commerce of the nation, and to add to its material wealth, and power, and strength, than any other enterprise since our history began. A tract of land greater than that of most of the empires of the world, has been reclaimed from a desert waste, and made a fertile valley, wherein may be grown all the products of the world, in quantities sufficient to sustain the entire human race. It has already added two States to our Union, populated the Territories both to the north and the south, has added hundreds of millions to the valuation of our country, and more than all, has created that feeling of common interest between the extreme East and West that will rivet forever the bands of union, and weld all into one common country, wherein all interests are forever to be the same. It has rendered that union secure, and has given inestimable blessings to every citizen of America.

Bright as may be the picture upon one side, it has likewise its dark side. Reputations have been ruined, and names once honored now lie in the seclusion of disgrace and infamy. Its purposes have been misunderstood, it has been tossed hither and thither, and has been made a foot-ball to be kicked about by politicians of all parties. Should its true object and purpose ever become appreciated, it will be looked upon as a corporation that has been of incalculable benefit to our country. The disgrace that has been placed upon one of its principal men will pass away, and in the clear light of the sun of truth and justice, the name of Oakes Ames will stand out bright and fair, as pure as the driven snow that circles around the base of the monument that has been erected to his memory on the highest point where the road he built crosses the Rocky mountains.

www.ingramcontent.com/pod-product-compliance
Lightning Source LLC
Chambersburg PA
CBHW021837230426
43669CB00008B/995